Pamper Yo

Pooch

Pamper Your Pooch

Sarah Whitehead

hamlyn

First published in Great Britain in 2007 by Hamlyn,
a division of Octopus Publishing Group Ltd,
2–4 Heron Quays, London E14 4JP

Sarah Whitehead asserts the moral right to be
identified as the author of this work.

All text written by Sarah Whitehead and Karen
Moore except for pages 22–23 (Ann Lees), pages
70–73 and 86–101 (Ryan O'Meara), pages 75–76
(Jill Blair) and pages 77–85 (Julia Robertson).

The recipes on pages 34–45 originally appeared in
Dog Treats, also published by Hamlyn.

ISBN-13: 978-0-600-61558-3

ISBN-10: 0-600-61558-8

A CIP catalogue record for this book is available
from the British Library

Printed and bound in China

10 9 8 7 6 5 4 3 2 1

The advice given in this book should not be used
as a substitute for that of a veterinary surgeon.

No dogs were harmed in the making of this book.

Unless the information given in this book is
specifically for female dogs, dogs are referred to
throughout as 'he'. The information is equally
applicable to both male and female dogs, unless
otherwise specified.

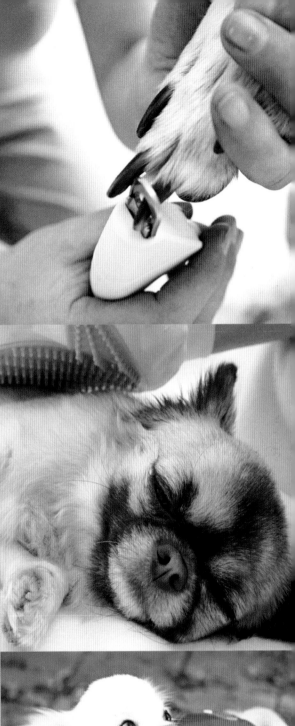

Contents

Introduction 6

A dog's life 10

Home sweet home 20

Doggy dining 30

The weekly workout 46

The pooch parlour 60

The New Age hound 74

The puppy inside 96

The dog about town 110

Index 126

Acknowledgements 128

Introduction

Dogs offer us so much through their love and companionship that there should be no doubt about their right to be pampered. Their love for us is unconditional, and we need to let them know how much we appreciate them. Taking the trouble to learn what your dog needs and the best ways to pamper him will raise his level of happiness and help him enjoy his life to the full.

YOU AND YOUR DOG

Humans and dogs have shared their lives for thousands of years, either in their homes as companions and friends or as working partners. This most rewarding of relationships is based on mutual understanding, trust and love. In order to achieve this relationship with your own dog, you will need to take the time to find out about him and his individual temperament and personality. Try looking at life from your dog's point of view to get a real insight in to how he thinks and what he wants.

It used to be thought that animals do not experience emotions, but over the last ten years or so it has been acknowledged that dogs do have emotions that we can recognize. For those of us who live with a dog, or several dogs, it's obvious that they can feel anger, frustration, sadness, pleasure, happiness and excitement, and knowing that dogs experience these feelings makes it even more important that we give them the best in life.

DOGS ARE NOT HUMAN

Dogs are great at reading their owner's body language and even facial expressions. Indeed, they are so sensitive to changes that they can warn of the onset of epileptic seizures, detect the early signs of illness and, of course, tell when their owner just needs a cuddle. This ability to 'read' us is one of the reasons dogs have found an enduring place in our homes and our hearts.

However, it is also this apparent ability to 'feel' for us that can make it appear that dogs have the same needs and values as we do. This is clearly not the case. We might regard a luxurious holiday as one that involves lying by a pool with a drink in one hand and a book in the other with nothing to do. Our dog, however, might well choose the complete opposite. All dogs love to express natural canine behaviours: running, barking, chasing, chewing, rolling and digging.

Just imagine if your dog could choose his own luxury holiday. Given the chance, a doggy spa day might possibly include mud bathing, rolling in highly malodorous substances and eating undesirable foods of the type that are usually found only under bushes. Although we might like our pets to smell of shampoo, they generally have other ideas.

You have to realize that what makes you happy will not necessarily please your dog, and taking the time to find out what makes him happy and then providing that pampering service is what will set you apart from the average owner.

Pampering your pet demands a compromise between human values, beliefs and practicalities and the genuine stuff of canine fantasy. We need to be able to lavish love and attention on our dogs while still allowing them to be dogs, rather than playthings. Owners who truly want the best for their pet need to be able to balance both and to do much more than just meet the dog's basic needs. But they also need to have some fun along the way.

This book is intended to be the equivalent of a wish list for both you and your dog. Why not make it his birthday every day?

Does your dog deserve pampering?

Everyone deserves to be able to spend some time on themselves now and then, and the same is true for your dog. There is no need to be embarrassed about the idea of doing what is best for your beloved pooch – after all, can you really put a price on unconditional love, affection and companionship?

WHAT YOUR DOG DOES FOR YOU

Extensive research has been carried out into the emotional and physical benefits of keeping a dog. Stroking a dog has been shown to reduce humans' blood pressure and heart rates. In addition, dog owners have been found to be generally more healthy than people who do not own a dog, as they suffer from fewer minor illnesses such as colds.

Interestingly, owners of dogs also seem to be happier about life in general, reporting a lower incidence of depression. And for those people who live alone, dogs can provide not only companionship, but also a structure to the day through the routine of caring for their needs.

Dogs can enhance the quality of life of those who own them, and boost their confidence with their unconditional loyalty and constant companionship. They can even be used to help teach shy children how to play and communicate with their peers.

KEEP IT IN THE FAMILY

Your dog is a recognized and important member of the family. We would not think twice about buying a special present for our partner or

spending time with our children, so it should be no different for our dog.

Dogs are loyal, generous creatures, providing company, friendship and a non-judgemental listening ear. There is nothing quite like coming home to a dog at the end of a hard day and being met enthusiastically by a friend who loves you unconditionally. Your dog is always pleased to see you, always willing to play but equally content just to be near you. He will probably pick up on your moods, quietly sitting and listening to the woes of the day, then cheerfully running and jumping when you are more inclined to join in with his zest for life.

LOVE FOR FREE
Finally, pampering your pet needn't break the bank. Indeed, there is plenty you can do for him that is completely free. If you were able to ask your dog what he really wanted in life, he would undoubtedly choose love and attention from you. And you can certainly find time for that.

A dog's life

Just as humans feel the need to be pampered from time to time, so do our dogs. And why not? They are an essential part of our family, and we should treat them as such. All dogs need to feel loved to be happy, so spend time with your dog by exercising him, playing with him, grooming him and generally making him feel like the centre of your world.

What your dog needs from you

All dogs need to be cared for both physically and emotionally, no matter what their breed, size, shape, colour or age. We all know the basics – food, exercise, grooming and regular veterinary check-ups – but what more can we do to make sure that they have not just a good life, but a luxurious one?

DINNER IS SERVED

We are what we eat, and this is also true for our dogs. Simply popping down to the supermarket and buying the first dog food you see on the shelf can be a recipe for digestive disaster. Choose your pet's food with as much care as you would your own. Check the list of ingredients to make sure that the food is made from natural products and avoid foods that contain a high ratio of cheap bulking agents, such as cereals.

Good-quality bought foods, whether you choose canned products or dry ones, are designed to meet the average dog's nutritional requirement. The pampered pooch, however, deserves more than this, and on pages 34–45 you will find recipes for homemade treats and rewards as well as some basic meals that will show your dog how much you care.

FITNESS FIRST

All dogs love exercise, and it's something that we need to provide in abundance. Dogs need to get out and about every day to stimulate both their minds and their bodies, and regular exercise will keep them – and us – in shape. Like all exercise plans, forming a routine and sticking to it is the best way to make sure it becomes part of your daily pattern.

Those who play together stay together, and playing with your dog is a wonderful form of exercise. There are plenty of toys available on the market. Some of these are designed for your dog to play with on his own, and others for you to play with together. See pages 46–57 for some ideas for both everyday walks and more demanding exercises.

HEALTH MATTERS

Basic healthcare routines are essential for all dogs, and whether you have a pampered pooch or simply a canine best friend it's important to schedule regular check-ups with your vet. These will allow your vet to spot signs of illness early and to ensure that your dog has a long and healthy life.

Sometimes tackling the most basic issues – such as poor dental hygiene – can have dramatic effects on your dog's wellbeing, so don't delay if you suspect that something's wrong.

MIND GAMES

Training may sound like a chore, but it should be one of the most enjoyable parts of your dog's day. Most owners want their dog to behave themselves in the house, to walk well on the lead and to come back when called in the park. But when it comes to training, try to be creative. Your dog will love the attention that he is given during training – and, of course, the food treats and play rewards he gets for good behaviour. Just think how much you will be able to impress your friends if you can teach your dog to perform tricks on command – like fetching the remote control, rolling over or shaking your hand.

Improving your dog's life

Our priorities for a good life may be very different from our dog's. It's easy to make assumptions and to think that the type of house and daily routines that we like are the best ones for our dogs. Try to put yourself in your dog's place to understand exactly what it is that he wants and needs.

THE HOME ENVIRONMENT

Interior design and DIY is a burgeoning business, and most people have an idea of the style of house they would like to live in and how it should be furnished and decorated. Indeed, DIY and the choice of paint colour can trigger many a domestic dispute. But your dog really doesn't care whether the sofa is cream or blue. He will still want to get on it with muddy paws. It's the fact that it is comfortable that makes him want to lie on it.

Think about your own home from your dog's point of view. Wooden floors may look fashionable and may be easy to clean, but consider whether your dog finds them cool and comfortable or hard, uncomfortable and slippery to walk on.

PHYSICAL ACTIVITY

Some people are more active than others. There are those who enjoy going to the gym every day for a regular workout, while other people find that even the thought of walking to the local shops fills them with dread. Dogs are different. All dogs love exercise, and it is something we need to be prepared to provide for them.

Even people who like to go to the gym every day do not just work on the same piece of equipment each time. Like people, dogs will get bored if they go on the same walks day in, day out. Vary your dog's exercise routines to help make his life more fulfilled. See some of the ideas for different activities and games on pages 46–57 so that you can keep your dog active and interested in what is going on around him.

MENTAL ACTIVITY

Our brains need to be kept working in the same way that the muscles of our bodies need to be kept in shape. Research increasingly indicates that under-utilizing brain power may result in a serious and permanent lack of cognitive development. The same is true of dogs. Just as we like to stretch ourselves with a crossword puzzle or sudoku, a dog will enjoy games that make him think and use all his senses. As well as varying your regular walks, try teaching your dog some new games and tricks (see pages 102–107).

PARK LIFE

Just as meeting your friends is a fundamental part of your social life, so your dog enjoys meeting other dogs. It is vitally important for him to be able to mix with other dogs regularly because it will help him develop his social skills and allow him to practise his inherent canine communication. Mixing and meeting with many new people and dogs also provides stimulation and fun and can lead to new friendships for the both of you.

BEDTIME

When it's time to go to bed, most of us prefer to be in a quiet, darkened room and to have a warm, comfortable bed that is raised off the ground. Dogs are very similar to us in this respect. They love peace and quiet while they are sleeping in their own bed. Don't expect your dog to sleep well if he is in a cardboard box in a busy kitchen.

Is your dog happy?

We all want our dogs to be happy, but how can we really tell if that is the case? When we are with other people we rely on smiles and words to find out how they are feeling, but dogs cannot communicate in these ways. However, they are the masters in reading and reacting to body language, so we need to learn from them.

THE WAG SAYS IT ALL

Tail wagging simply means friendliness and contentment, doesn't it? Well, nearly. In general, a mid-height, mid-speed wag will indicate friendliness. The majority of genuinely sociable dogs lower their tails slightly when they greet people, but the excitement of greeting can be so great for some dogs that their tails go round and round, windmill style. Other dogs seem to 'wag' their whole body. If the tail is tucked between a dog's legs he may be experiencing fear or anxiety, even if it is still wagging.

CANINE SMILES

It is natural for humans to think of a smile when describing a person showing happiness. Dogs can smile too. The corners of a dog's mouth are drawn right back, and they may even be drawn into an upward curve, just like a human grin. Dalmatians and Golden Retrievers are classic 'smilers'. However, if your dog is showing his teeth, he may be telling you to back off.

THE EARS HAVE IT

A dog's ears are an excellent barometer of his feelings. Ears that are up and alert often indicate excitement, confidence or assertion, while ears that are held back and down usually indicate fear. Ears turned almost inside out can show exuberance and flirtation. Some breeds can be more difficult to read than others, however. Cocker Spaniels, for example, always look sad, with those doleful eyes and long, drooping ears, so you may have to look for other clues.

PLAY WITH ME

A happy dog is one that wants to play. Your dog will invite you to play by offering a 'play bow' (see opposite). His front end will be lowered with his bottom in the air, and his ears will stand up. Your dog may only hold this position briefly before breaking off and running in some random direction, so keep an eye out for it. The play bow may be accompanied by excited barking.

LUST FOR LIFE

The easiest way to tell if your dog is happy is by observing his overall demeanour. Although a dog will lie at rest when there is

Telltale signs

A happy and contented dog will have...	An unhappy dog may...
• a relaxed body posture	• be slouched rather than relaxed
• ears that are up but not forward	• be uninterested in food
• a head that is held high and a mouth that is slightly open with the tongue exposed	• show little enthusiasm for daily activities, such as walking, playing or general family life
• a 'loose' stance, with his weight flat on all four feet	• take himself off on his own all day, away from the rest of the family
• a tail that is down and relaxed or horizontal and gently wagging	

nothing interesting going on, as soon as his lead is produced, he should spring into life at a moment's notice. A happy dog is an enthusiastic and energetic dog, ready to take on almost any challenge, from daily walks to agility classes or learning some tricks.

To give your dog the very best in life, why not try dividing his daily activities in a pie chart? If each hour of his day is represented by one segment, how many segments of your dog's day are filled with pleasurable activities that enrich his life compared to simply sleeping, or waiting for you to come home from a hard day at work? Make a list of all the different activities that your dog loves doing and then estimate how much of his time is spent engaged in those activities. If you find a deficit, you know that you need to take action! For example, we all know that dogs love their food. If eating takes up only a tiny fraction of your dog's day, why not work on ways to make the experience last longer? You will find some helpful suggestions on pages 104–105.

Have a think about what would make your dog's day perfect, then take steps to make it a reality!

What makes different breeds happy?

Think about the sort of interaction you have with your dog and consider whether he really enjoys it. Not all dogs are the same, and different breeds have different needs. If your dog is a crossbreed, think about the kinds of breed influences in his genetic make-up. This will give you an idea of the kind of activities that will make him happy.

TERRIER TYPES

What makes terrier types happy? Well, just think about what they were bred to do. Most terrier breeds, such as Jack Russells and West Highland Terriers, were developed to hunt for vermin, chase them and even dig them out from underground. Even if your dog isn't a pure-bred terrier, if he has some of this go-getting blood in his heritage he's bound to love terrier-type activities.

- **Digging** Get out a spade and create a digging pit in the garden for your dog. Use play sand to fill it so that his paws don't get dirty, and hide his favourite toys in the bottom so that he learns to hunt for treasure.

- **Chasing** Get a long tug rope and whiz it around the floor. Make sure that you can get the toy back safely at the end of the game by swapping it for a titbit.
- **Killing games** These may sound blood-thirsty, but as long as predatory 'shake the toy' games are directed at fluffy toys from the pet shop, no one should get hurt.
- **Agility classes** Even though he may be small, don't think that your dog won't enjoy an activity like agility training (see page 52).
- **Tricks** Terriers love to spend time with their owners, so put this time to good use by teaching your dog some tricks (see pages 106–107) – he'll love it, and his talents will impress your friends.

GUNDOG GAMES

Gundogs love to retrieve, of course, but many also like to run and stalk their prey, and they all love attention and cuddles. These dogs, which include some spaniels and Labradors, tend to be very responsive to their surroundings, and, almost universally, they also love water – the muddier the better.

- **Swimming** Provide a paddling pool for your dog, especially on warm days, so that he can paddle or even wallow in the water if the mood takes him. Include opportunities for safe swimming when you are devising your programme of weekly walks.
- **Retrieving** Provide lots of toys, especially soft ones, for your gundog to mouth and carry around. If you don't, he'll pick up the remote control or your mobile phone instead.
- **Stalking and running** Chase games and hide-and-seek appeal to these dogs' hunting instincts and to their sense of humour.
- **Eating** Most gundogs are real foodies. Help prevent them overeating by giving them food little and often. Use treats in training to make them really happy.

HERDING HAPPINESS

Of course, a herd of cattle, a flock of sheep or a gaggle of geese would make most herding types ecstatic, but not many of us have access to these in daily life, especially if we live in large towns or cities. Dogs such as Collies, with herding genes in their make-up, love to chase, round up and sometimes nip at the heels of pretend 'sheep', such as joggers and cyclists in the local park, so it's important that we give them a chance to express this behaviour – without them getting into trouble!

- **Chasing** This activity needs to be fast and furious, so get a ball catapult or use a tennis racquet to get a ball really flying through the air. Repeat the action as many times as your dog will chase – herders love repeated patterns of behaviour.
- **Herding** Teach your herder to do a food circuit (see pages 50–51) to combine chasing food and running in a herding pattern.
- **Brainpower** Your herding dog needs to use his brain to solve puzzles (see pages 104–105), and these breeds are happiest when they are being trained, as long as the training methods used are fun and enjoyable.

HOUNDS

Hounds are among the most ancient breeds of dog and have changed little over the centuries. There are two main types, distinguished by how they locate their prey – scent hounds and sight hounds. Scent hounds, such as Beagles and Dachshunds, were bred for their stamina; sight hounds, such as Greyhounds and Whippets, were bred for their speed and agility. Scent hounds can be rather vocal at times, and you may find you have a natural 'singer' on your hands. Sight hounds are often quieter and have more sensitive natures, so they may not appreciate some of the more boisterous games that scent hounds enjoy.

- **Tracking** As their name suggests, scent hounds love to use their noses. This makes tracking of any sort a favourite pastime (see page 50). Some hounds can be hard to recall once they have their nose to a scent, so if you keep your hound on lead make sure he doesn't miss out on the fun by looking at some of the suggestions on pages 56–57.
- **Running** Sight hounds love to run. Many dog racing tracks now host open days for the public, to which anyone can take their dog, no matter what breed, and have a go at running around the track.

TOY DOGS

These dogs originally come from a variety of working backgrounds. Some come from terrier ancestry (such as the Yorkshire Terrier), others have gundog blood (the King Charles Spaniel) and some are from a hound background (the Italian Greyhound). However, all toy dogs have been bred to be smaller than their ancestors and to provide companionship. They tend to be plucky and courageous and can make good guard dogs. Although they are very small and do not require vast amounts of exercise, toy dogs are surprisingly energetic.

Keeping busy

Research on human happiness has concluded that as well as a good environment, people are happiest when they are fully occupied doing a job that they excel at. When this happens, time flies and people feel content with themselves and their lives. Your dog, too, needs to be occupied with activities he enjoys and does well, so spend some time finding out what makes your dog feel fulfilled.

CROSSBREEDS AND MONGRELS

Not everyone owns a specific breed of dog, and there are many dogs of unknown parentage. If you have one of these dogs you'll have to do a little more work to find out what it is that your dog finds fun. Look for clues to his ancestry in his appearance and behaviour and then try some of the alternative activities described on pages 52–55, or have a go at some unusual games (see pages 102–103) or puzzles (see pages 104–105) to see what really makes your dog happy.

OTHER BREEDS

Other breeds may not easily fit into any category. In order to understand what makes your particular dog truly happy, you need to know what it was originally bred to do. You may then need to use your imagination to offer your dog an activity that he thinks is truly wonderful. Dalmatians were bred to trot behind horse-drawn carriages to protect their masters from highwaymen; Boxers were bred to hunt boar and bear; the Siberian Husky to pull sleds; and the German Shepherd Dog to herd and guard sheep.

Home sweet home

All dogs need time and space to rest and be quiet when they're at home, and this is particularly important if you have young children. So that your dog can relax completely when he needs to, you must consider important factors such as where he eats and sleeps, and also whether the noise levels and general home environment could be modified to improve his quality of life. It is important for every dog to live in a happy, loving home that he can call his own, but it is equally important that there is an area within the home that really is just his.

The perfect home

Most dogs are able to adapt well to whatever family life throws at them, but you will save yourself a lot of trouble and your dog a lot of anguish if you know your dog and what type of life he will enjoy. Boisterous breeds, such as Staffordshire Bull Terriers, often love an active family home with plenty going on, but smaller, quieter breeds, such as Yorkshire Terriers, may prefer a comfortable lap to sleep on instead.

EATING IN PEACE

Food is one of the major highlights of your dog's day. Most of the time your dog will be fed his food from a bowl, and it is important that he can eat in peace. After all, if you had looked forward to a special meal all day, you wouldn't want it to be spoiled by having someone standing looking over your shoulder the whole time. So, make sure there is no harassment from adults, children or other pets, which could lead to food guarding and aggression, or bolting food, which can cause indigestion.

Find a quiet corner of the house – the kitchen is usually best so that spillages can be quickly mopped up – and make sure no one disturbs your dog while he eats.

FORTY WINKS

Dogs spend a lot of their time sleeping. Indeed, one of the main attractions of having a dog as a pet is his ability to rest when he is not being entertained and then to leap into action at the first indication that a walk is in the offing or when the toy box is opened.

Make sure your dog has somewhere quiet to sleep. Some dogs may still insist on sleeping in the middle of the kitchen floor while Mum is cooking and the children are playing at the kitchen table, but they should still have the option to go to bed in a quiet room if they prefer.

QUIET PLEASE

Dogs have sensitive ears, as anyone who has tried to sneak a biscuit out of the tin without their dog hearing will know only too well, even if the dog was at the bottom of the garden at the time. Noisy music, shouting and screaming children may upset some dogs, particularly those that are more sensitive to sounds, such as Border Collies. Although some breeds – Boxers and Labradors, for example – seem better able to cope with the noises of everyday life, remember that they too will appreciate a bit of peace and quiet at times.

NEW ADDITIONS

Be considerate to your old dog if you decide to get a new puppy (see page 109). There can be nothing worse than being pestered by a canine newcomer, and it will affect the two dogs' long-term relationship if the newcomer's tiresome behaviour is not controlled. Continue to lavish on your old dog the love and attention that he has learned to expect.

Feng shui and your dog

Originating in China thousands of years ago, feng shui has the basic premise that our environment affects our health and wellbeing. Applying a few simple rules to the living space can create a home in which the occupants feel secure, nurtured and happy. Humans may have more complex requirements than animals, but the principle is the same: if you are in command of your living space, other aspects of your life will benefit from the confidence you feel.

WILL FENG SHUI HELP YOUR DOG?

Following a few simple guidelines when you are selecting a suitable area for your dog's bed will ensure that he feels like a valued and secure member of the family. Just as people have their favourite chairs, your dog needs to feel that there is a particular area in the home that belongs exclusively to him.

The guiding principle in this aspect of feng shui is to place the person or animal 'in command' of their personal space. By so doing they feel confident and relaxed in their home, and if we consider a well-placed armchair the reasoning becomes clearer and can be more easily transferred to your dog's bed. The high back of an easy chair offers a sense of protection, as do the raised arms, and the combination of both makes it a more attractive location in which to relax or take a nap. If the chair is located facing into the room and offers a view of the door, the chances of being startled by someone entering are reduced. An area free from furniture in front of the armchair allows you to stretch your legs or move in and out easily, so coffee tables and the like should be placed to the side. In short, the armchair and immediate area around it become your 'space'.

If the area set aside for your dog conforms to feng shui guidelines he will:

- Sleep soundly without risk of being disturbed by passing feet.
- Have an area to which he can safely retreat when he is tired or feeling unwell.
- Be certain of his place within the family group, benefiting from the assurance this brings to his daily life.

Basic principles

Feng shui advises that you use the following guidelines when you are selecting the best position for your dog's bed.

• A location in which your dog is close to the rest of the family or those he considers part of his 'pack', but somewhere that is not immediately next to noisy machinery, such as a dishwasher.

• A solid wall behind his basket to give a feeling of safety.

• A view of the doors through which people will enter or leave the room.

• Protection on each side in the form of an infrequently used cupboard, to shield against people passing too closely when he is sleeping; alternatively, select a position in the corner of the room.

• A clear area to the front of the basket so that he can enter and exit the space without having to overcome obstacles.

• Food and water bowls placed close to, but not in front of, the basket so that he can eat and drink without disturbance.

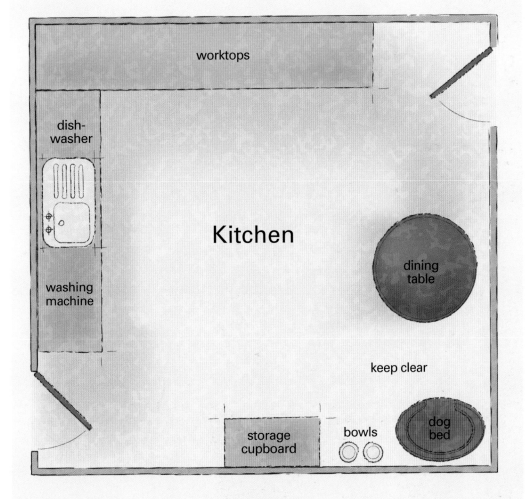

The perfect bed

The ideal bed for your dog will be comfy, warm and just the right size and shape. You, however, will also want something that is aesthetically pleasing and that suits your home. There is a wide choice of beds, but before you buy consider the options carefully, and don't forget that you may need to consult your dog.

Whatever type of bed you choose for your dog, make sure that he will be secure and warm when using it. The bed should be a little bigger than he is and allow enough space for him to turn around comfortably.

TRADITIONAL STYLES

An oval or round rigid plastic style of bed is economical, easy to clean and almost indestructible. A duvet, plush cushion or cosy blanket should be placed inside to make it more

comfortable, and it is even possible to buy heated underblankets to take the chill off the bed on chilly winter nights, although these should not be left on all night.

Woven wicker baskets may look great, but they are not only tempting to chew but can also be difficult to clean and disinfect properly. If you do choose a wicker basket, scrub it with soapy hot water regularly and put it outside to dry in the fresh air.

Older dogs often find that a beanbag filled with polystyrene beads offers warmth, comfort and support. These have the advantage that they do not harbour parasites. Buy one with the strongest inner cover you can find and that allows you to top up the filling with extra beads. Make sure that it has a washable top cover. Before you buy a beanbag, however, be honest with yourself. If you think there is the slightest chance that your dog will chew his bed, choose something else. Can you imagine how long it would take to pick up thousands of tiny polystyrene balls that have been scattered about your home?

MODERN TIMES

There are numerous designs of modern dog beds, ranging from soft beds that come in every imaginable shape and size with a variety of patterns, colours and fabrics to choose from, to beds that look like sofas, chaise longues or four-poster beds. You can even find doggy hammocks for a real treat on long, hot, summer days. An older dog might appreciate an orthopaedic support. The contoured pillow is designed to provide maximum support and restful sleep for your dog by correctly supporting his head, neck and jaw.

Most of the more exotic and unusual styles are available only through the internet or mail order. Before you buy, think about how much space the bed will take up and whether it will be practical in your house. Also, consider whether you will be able to keep it hygienic.

SAFE AND SECURE

Crates are becoming an increasingly popular alternative to the traditional dog bed. They are made of wire panels that can be folded flat for moving. The dog's natural instincts are to find a den, a place that offers protection, and many dogs take naturally to the crate if it is introduced gradually. They become a sanctuary, providing your dog with total security and comfort. Lining it with a washable fur-fabric rug or cushion will make it more appealing. Encourage your dog to go in by placing some tasty treats or favourite toys inside. The crate will serve your dog all his life: on holidays, when you go visiting and when your dog is ill and needs protection, nursing and rest. Don't forget, you can always decorate the outside to blend in with your home furnishings, your taste and your dog's personality.

Travelling in style

Families enjoy spending their leisure time together, whether it is a special day out or an extended holiday, so why not take your dog with you? More and more places now welcome dogs, so you should make sure he arrives safely and in style, no matter what mode of transport you choose.

SAFETY AND COMFORT

Most dogs have to make journeys by car, even if it is just to the vet for a check-up or regular vaccinations. All dogs should be secured in the car behind a dog guard, in a crate or by a specially designed car harness. Pop-up tents that fit into the boot of your car are now available – they are less cumbersome than a rigid crate.

Just like people, some dogs suffer from travel sickness, sometimes to the point of not wanting to get in the car at all. If your dog is generally happy to go in the car but is sometimes sick, there are a few simple things you can do to make sure he will enjoy the journey:

- Do not feed him before the journey.
- Give him half a ginger biscuit before the journey, which will settle his stomach.
- Try to position him so that he cannot see out of the window because the chances of motion sickness are reduced if your dog cannot see the outside world whizzing past.

If your dog is unwilling to get in the car at all, there are a few things you can do to help:

- Make the car a welcoming place to be while it is stationary by giving your dog his meals there or by offering some favourite treats.
- Get your dog used to the car by taking him on a few short journeys and always returning home to a game.
- Gradually build up to longer journeys that again always end in a great walk or a game rather than a bath or a trip to the vet.

PERFECT DAYS OUT

It may seem obvious, but before you set out with your dog make sure that you check that he will be welcome at your destination. Some guidebooks include this type of information, and the websites of many attractions will indicate if dogs are allowed.

There may well be occasions in your dog's life when taking public transport is essential. This experience has the potential to be noisy, over-crowded and overwhelming for your dog's sense of smell and personal space. If your dog is small enough, a pet carrier may be the answer. It will keep him out of harm's way and will allow him to rest during the journey. However, larger dogs will have to learn to cope with the hustle and bustle, the strange movements and sounds – and the likelihood that people will want to stop and say hello!

The best way to help your dog with these situations is to acclimatize him to them while he is still young. Take your puppy out and about and enjoy the experience together. He will soon learn that, however strange and unfamiliar the experience, you will always be there by his side. You may have forgotten how much pleasure can be drawn from riding on top of an open-top bus in a tourist town or taking a trip to do some sightseeing by rail. Make it fun and your dog will enjoy it too!

There are many places that you and your dog can visit together. Some churches, castles and open-air museums are open to all members of the family. How about a cross-country walk or even a tour of a local city or town?

With no entrance fee to pay at all, a trip to the beach can be great fun. Do bear in mind that not all beaches permit dogs all year round, so check before you go. There is something about the open space, the salt in the air, the wind and the seaweed that leave a dog quivering with excitement as he races to the surf, even if he doesn't actually want to go in the water. By the end of the day you will have a very happy – and very tired – dog to take home.

If you are out all day you will need to eat. Some restaurants will allow your dog entry as well, but no doubt he will always help with any leftovers from your picnic.

ABOUT TOWN

When you are travelling about town with your dog you have a number of options. You might decide to walk or take public transport together, or you might prefer to transport your dog in style. There are some great pet carriers available for smaller dogs, from the practical – a crate on wheels – to the stylish – a dog carrier that can be coordinated to suit your own outfit. Whichever option you choose, your dog's comfort should always be your first consideration.

HOLIDAY SEASON

There is no reason why your dog should not be included in the annual family holiday, and there are even some specialist travel agencies that will help coordinate holidays for both you and your canine pal. There are plenty of hotels that accept dogs, and you should look on the Internet for information. Be aware that even if a hotel welcomes dogs it may not actually allow them in the guests' rooms but only in on-site kennels instead. If you prefer a more home-from-home environment for your dog, some self-catering holiday cottages usually accept dogs, while the more adventurous might be drawn to a caravan or camping holiday.

TRAVELLING ABROAD

The introduction of pet passports in some countries has made it possible for dogs to travel to a number of other countries. To help make your dog's journey from one place to another as comfortable as possible you should:

- Make sure that your dog is fit and healthy before he travels.
- Do not feed him immediately before travelling.
- Allow him the opportunity to go to the toilet before he goes in his carrying container.
- Let him get used to his crate before you travel, so he is happy to be in it.
- Make sure the crate he is travelling in is spacious and well ventilated.
- Make sure your dog will have access to water throughout the entire trip.
- Put a favourite blanket or cushion in the crate to provide him with a little extra comfort.

Before you plan the holiday, check that your dog's vaccinations are up to date and that you have the relevant vaccination documentation from your veterinary surgeon.

Take a seat

While most airlines will accept dogs only if they are in secure crates in the hold, a few exclusive companies will arrange for your dog to have his own seat. But be prepared to pay for the privilege and don't expect the same in-flight services for your pet as you would expect for yourself!

FLIGHT COMMANDER

Some airline companies now actively encourage owners to take their dogs on holiday with them, and one has even launched a frequent-flier incentive, allowing dogs to earn points when they accompany their owners abroad. Once they have completed their first flight, they receive a complementary gift of a doggy T-shirt and sparkly tags. The airline has opened an exclusive pet reception centre at Heathrow Airport, London, which provides a full feeding and grooming service to help your dog recover from jetlag and relax once he is back on home soil.

IN-FLIGHT ACCESSORIES

If your dog is a frequent overseas visitor, why not treat him to his own leather passport holder? With his picture and documentation enclosed, he'll look every bit the seasoned traveller.

Doggy dining

All dogs need good, healthy food, and just as we know
that we are what we eat, so we are becoming increasingly
aware that what we feed our pets has a direct bearing not
only on their health but also on their behaviour. Choosing
your dog's food carefully and feeding regularly are
essential, but it's also a plus to offer little treats and
special meals from time to time.

What, where and when

Dog food is usually available wet (in a can) or dry (in bags, sacks and boxes). Price and convenience may be the factors that govern your choice, but it is essential that you know what's actually in the food you are giving your dog.

Commercial pet foods are of two types: complete and complementary. Many canned foods are complementary, which means that they require an additional mix of biscuits or meal to add bulk to the diet and balance their components. Most dried foods are complete, which means additional food is not required – in fact, adding to them can upset the nutritional balance of the food. There are also products for life stages such as puppyhood and old age, and some companies even produce diets for conditions such as kidney disease and obesity. These need to be fed under veterinary guidance.

Most dogs like to be fed twice a day, and this regime encourages the effective working of the digestive system and helps to balance your dog's blood sugar levels. Being hungry can make dogs irritable and grumpy – and such mood swings can be avoided by feeding little and often.

Giving human food to dogs is a contentious issue. Who can resist those big, sorrowful eyes? However, biscuits and sweets manufactured for people make dogs pile on the calories and add to the risk of tooth decay. Treats made especially for dogs are a better idea and can also be used as training rewards. However, always be careful to ensure you do not overfeed your dog.

All the recipes in this chapter include food that is safe for your dog to eat, but different foods can affect dogs in different ways. Start by giving small amounts of a recipe, and you will quickly discover what your dog's favourite is.

Some foods that are fine for humans can be harmful if given to dogs. Chocolate meant for humans is toxic for dogs, even in cakes or as an ingredient in other dishes. Dogs are unable to deal with the theobromine it contains and have been known to die after eating a box of chocolates intended for human consumption. If you want to give your dog something sweet, look out for specially prepared dog chocolates, which contain very low levels of theobromine and are therefore safe for dogs to eat. Large quantities of grapes or raisins may also upset your dog's digestion, so offer these with caution.

ACTIVE DOG OR COUCH POTATO?

Dogs need to be fed according to their lifestyle. Owners are often under the illusion that just because they own a working breed it must be fed a working dog's diet. However, dogs that are genuinely active for eight hours a day will clearly need different food, in both quantity and type, from a less active dog of the same breed.

quality ingredients when you are buying food for your dog – and give junk food a miss.

Knowing what's best for your pet can be a confusing business, especially if you want to feed a prepared commercial food. If your dog suffers regularly from one or more of the following, it may indicate his food is not suiting him.

- Inconsistent digestion, which may take the form of your dog having a runny tummy from time to time.
- Flatulence, which is unpleasant for both you and the dog.
- Intolerances to certain food components or allergic reactions to irritants such as fleas or grass pollen.
- Smelly, frequent, large motions – the amount should be what you would expect from a dog of his size.
- Failure to gain weight despite eating well.
- Over- or under-activity. Owners often describe a 'mad half-hour', which usually occurs in the evening about an hour after the dog's meal, when the dog hares around the sitting room using the sofa as a springboard. Even long walks fail to wear the dog out and he is constantly on the alert.
- Eating unusual things, such as soil, grass, plants, paper tissue, sticks and stones.
- Eating his own faeces.
- Rubbing, nibbling or scratching at his feet, stomach and base of tail or face.

H₂O FOR HEALTH

It is vital that fresh water is available for your dog at all times, whether you provide bottled water or fill your dog's bowl from the tap. Fluids are essential to a dog's wellbeing, ensuring that nutrients are carried through the body effectively and that wastes are eliminated, so whether you are providing your dog with wet or dry food, a bowl of fresh drinking water should always be readily available for him to wash it down with. Proprietary water fountains, which provide fresh, clean water for your dog on demand, are a wonderful way of encouraging him to maintain a healthy intake.

KNOW THE ENEMY

Like people, different dogs have different nutritional requirements. Just as some people can't eat nuts or strawberries, so dogs can react badly to certain ingredients in their food. However, you don't need to be a kitchen slave to give your pet the very best. Follow the guidelines of top chefs: use the freshest, best-

Warning

Feeding cooked bones of any kind can be very dangerous for your pet. Shards of bone can do internal damage, and dogs often break their teeth when they are crunching them.

SUPERSIZED DOGS

Too much of a good thing will lead to obesity, which is an increasingly common problem for dogs. You need to be aware of both the nutritional content and the calorific value of your dog's food. Overweight dogs are unfit and incapable of leading an active life. In some breeds excess weight may lead to respiratory problems, but in all breeds, joints and internal organs have excess demands put on them if the dog is carrying extra weight, which can lead to arthritis and heart problems.

When you touch your dog, you should be able to feel his ribs just beneath the skin (see below). If you have to dig around for them, your dog is probably overweight. If in doubt, take your dog to the vet, who will be able to weigh him for you and score his body condition.

If any of these signs sound familiar it may be worth experimenting with other foods. Some owners try three or four types of food before they find one that suits their dog. If you decide to change your dog's food, make sure that you do it gradually over about five days, as a sudden change in food can cause a stomach upset.

Healthy snacks for training

You know that the way to your dog's heart is through his stomach. When you want to reward your dog during training, praise him for standing still when he is being groomed or just let him know how much you love him, give him one of the following tasty alternatives to shop-bought treats.

Makes about 10 biscuits
Preparation time 15 minutes
Cooking time 40 minutes

¼ beef stock cube
1 tablespoon boiling water
1 tablespoon vegetable oil
½ small egg, beaten
25 g (1 oz) plain flour, plus extra for rolling
25 g (1 oz) plain wholemeal flour
25 g (1 oz) porridge oats
25 g (1 oz) cornmeal
6 brewer's yeast tablets, crushed, or 1 teaspoon brewer's yeast powder
1 tablespoon garlic powder

No-fleas-on-me fancies

Your dog will love these flapjacks and you needn't worry about feeding him any unwanted calories as long as you feed them sparingly, keeping them for a special treat.

1 Dissolve the stock cube in the boiling water and leave to cool.

2 Mix together the oil and egg and blend in the cooled stock.

3 Put all the dry ingredients in a bowl and mix together. Gradually add the stock mixture and work into a dough.

4 Roll out the dough on a lightly floured surface to about 5 mm (¼ inch) thick and use biscuit cutters to cut out shapes. Transfer them to a lightly greased baking sheet and cook in a preheated oven, 200°C (400°F), Gas Mark 6, for 40 minutes, or until golden-brown. Transfer to a wire rack to cool.

Apple snacks

Many dogs really enjoy fruit, and these little snacks are healthy and delicious. The slices are portable, so take them out on walks to reward fast recalls. You can even nibble one yourself when your energy begins to flag.

Makes 20–25 slices
Preparation time 5 minutes
Cooking time about 45 minutes

1 dessert apple

1 Wash and core the apple and slice it as thinly as you can. Arrange the slices, without overlapping them, on a nonstick baking sheet.

2 Put the tray on the lowest shelf in a pre-heated oven, 140°C (275°F), Gas Mark 1, and bake for about 45 minutes, or until the slices are light brown and crispy. Turn two or three times while cooking to make sure the apple cooks evenly.

3 Transfer the crisp slices to a wire rack to cool, then store in an airtight container.

Nutty mutt nibbles

These delicious, crumbly little treats will melt in his mouth and are the perfect reward for good behaviour. What more could any dog ask for?

Makes 10–12 balls
Preparation time 10 minutes
Cooking time 25 minutes

1 tablespoon shelled pecan nuts, coarsely chopped
1 tablespoon shelled walnuts, coarsely chopped
1 tablespoon peanuts
2 tablespoons plain wholemeal flour
125 g (4 oz) crunchy peanut butter

1 Mix all the ingredients together in a bowl.

2 Gently form pieces of the mixture into balls about 2.5 cm (1 inch) across by rolling them between the palms of your hands.

3 Place the balls on a nonstick baking sheet and cook in a preheated oven, 150°C (300°F), Gas Mark 2, for 25 minutes. Allow to cool on the baking sheet before handling or serving them.

Recipes for meals

Is your dog tired of having to eat the same food every day? You could try buying an alternative brand or a different flavour, but instead of looking along the supermarket shelves why not make something yourself? There's nothing like home-cooked food: you know exactly where the ingredients have come from and how the food has been prepared. More importantly, your dog will love having the chance to try something new.

Serves 1
Preparation time 5 minutes

1 wheat breakfast biscuit, crumbled
2 tablespoons bran strands
1 tablespoon bran flakes, crumbled
4 tablespoons low-fat natural yogurt
1 tablespoon liquid honey
thin slices of fruit, such as apple, banana, strawberries or mango, to decorate

Puppy pick-me-up

This is the perfect way for young dogs to start the day, or you could serve it to older dogs as a special treat. Add a few slices of your dog's favourite fresh fruit, ringing the changes with whatever is in season.

1 Mix together all of the ingredients and transfer them to a serving dish.

2 Decorate the mixture with slices of fruit and serve immediately.

Warning

If your dog has any special dietary requirement, such as a wheat allergy, check with your vet before feeding any of our special recipes.

Cool kebab

Kidneys can be rather rich, so do not serve this all at the same meal. Slide the cooked meat and vegetables from the skewer into a dish to serve. Cover and store in the refrigerator for a day or two.

Serves 4
Preparation time 10 minutes
Cooking time 15 minutes

325 g (11 oz) kidneys, quartered
6 cherry tomatoes, halved
8 button mushrooms

1 Arrange the kidneys and vegetables on one or more long skewer; those with a wooden handle will be easier to turn.

2 Cook the kebab under a preheated hot grill, turning frequently, until it is cooked through (the juices should run clear).

3 Allow to cool and store in the refrigerator until required.

Chunky chow

A filling meal for the health-conscious hound, this is a good way to make sure your dog has plenty of fibre. Parsley is a good breath-freshener for humans and dogs alike.

Serves 2
Preparation time 15 minutes, plus standing
Cooking time 15 minutes

125 g (4 oz) couscous
200 ml (7 fl oz) boiling water
1 teaspoon vegetable or olive oil
1 chicken stock cube
40 g (1½ oz) low-fat sunflower or vegetable spread
250 g (8 oz) turkey meat, diced
75 g (3 oz) canned chickpeas, drained and roughly chopped
25 g (1 oz) canned red kidney beans, drained and roughly chopped
¼ teaspoon garlic powder
1 tablespoon natural yogurt
1 tablespoon dried skimmed milk
sprig of parsley, to garnish

1 Put the couscous in a saucepan and add the boiling water, oil and crumbled stock cube. Stir, cover and leave to stand for 5 minutes.

2 Add 15 g (½ oz) sunflower or vegetable spread and cook gently over a medium heat for 3 minutes. Separate the couscous grains with a fork.

3 Melt the remaining sunflower or vegetable spread in another pan and add the turkey, chickpeas, kidney beans and garlic powder. Stir-fry until the meat has browned. Remove from the heat and stir in the yogurt and milk.

4 Spoon the couscous around the edge of a bowl and place the meat mixture in the middle. Leave to cool, then serve garnished with parsley.

Serves 1–2
Preparation time 20 minutes
Cooking time 30–35 minutes

500 g (1 lb) potatoes, quartered
1 beef stock cube
300 ml (½ pint) boiling water
250 g (8 oz) minced lean beef
50 g (2 oz) carrot, diced
¼ teaspoon dried parsley
¼ teaspoon dried thyme
1 tablespoon beef gravy
granules or powder
2 tablespoons grated hard cheese

Growling grub pie

The reaction from your dog when you put this tasty pie in front of him will more than repay the effort of making it. If you have a small dog, make two pies from these ingredients and freeze one for another day.

1 Bring a saucepan of water to the boil and cook the potatoes until they are soft. Drain and mash.

2 In a large frying pan dissolve the stock cube in the boiling water, then add the beef, carrot and herbs. Bring to the boil and simmer until soft. Add the gravy granules or powder to thicken, then pour into a lightly greased 1.2 litre (2 pint) ovenproof dish.

3 Spoon the potatoes on top of the meat and gently fork over to roughen the surface. Sprinkle over the cheese and bake in a preheated oven, 200°C (400°F), Gas Mark 6, for 20 minutes or until the cheese has melted. Brown under a preheated hot grill to form a crust, if required. Allow to cool before serving.

Scamp's stir-fry

If you are using a stock cube, check the ingredients because many stock cubes contain extra salt. If you make your own stock, make and freeze a few extra portions. Otherwise, look for some of the good-quality stocks available in supermarkets.

Serves 1–2
Preparation time 15 minutes
Cooking time 15–20 minutes

2 tablespoons vegetable oil

125 g (4 oz) boneless chicken (raw or cooked), roughly chopped

50 g (2 oz) spinach (fresh or frozen)

1 potato, diced

4 cherry tomatoes, quartered

2 green cabbage leaves, roughly chopped

1 carrot, chopped

1 teaspoon garlic powder

2 handfuls of your dog's favourite complementary mixer meal

125 ml (4 fl oz) chicken or beef stock

chopped parsley, to garnish

1 Heat the oil in a large, nonstick frying pan and add the chicken, vegetables and garlic powder. Cook over a high heat until the vegetables are tender.

2 Transfer the mixture to a large bowl and add the mixer meal. Add the stock and mix together.

3 Leave to cool and serve garnished with parsley.

Mutt's milky pudding

Use semi-skimmed milk or a mixture of half milk and half water in this easy rice pudding. Too much whole milk can upset delicate digestions.

Serves 1–2
Preparation time 15 minutes
Cooking time 2½–3 hours

600 ml (1 pint) semi-skimmed milk or half milk, half water

40 g (1½ oz) short-grain rice

25 g (1 oz) low-fat sunflower or vegetable spread

40 g (1½ oz) demerara sugar

pinch of grated nutmeg

1 Put the milk, rice, sunflower or vegetable spread and sugar in a lightly greased 1.2 litre (2 pint) ovenproof dish and sprinkle the nutmeg over the top.

2 Bake in a preheated oven, 150°C (300°F), Gas Mark 2, for 2½–3 hours, stirring twice during the first hour. Allow to cool before serving.

Recipes for treats

These recipes are suitable as an occasional treat for your dog rather than as part of his regular maintenance diet. You should be careful not to overfeed your dog, and should limit treats to 10 per cent of his daily food intake. However, sensible eating on a daily basis means we can all enjoy a little indulgence from time to time!

Serves 1
Preparation time 10 minutes
Cooking time 5 minutes

2 slices of wholemeal or brown bread
½ tablespoon low-fat sunflower or vegetable spread
1 tablespoon low-fat soft cheese
4 tablespoons flaked tuna or canned dog meat
1 tablespoon crunchy peanut butter

Top dog toasties

Brown bread, made with wholewheat or wholemeal flour, is better for dogs than white bread. Choose tuna in spring water because tuna preserved in brine is too salty for dogs.

1 Toast one side of the bread under a preheated hot grill until light golden-brown. Remove and turn the grill down to low.

2 Thinly spread the untoasted side of one slice of bread with sunflower or vegetable spread, then lavishly cover with soft cheese and tuna or dog meat. Thinly spread the untoasted side of the remaining slice of bread with peanut butter.

3 Sandwich the toast together and place back under the grill for a couple of minutes on each side until the toast is crisp and the filling has melted. Cut into halves, allow to cool and serve.

Makes about 12 balls
Preparation time 15 minutes,
plus standing
Cooking time 20 minutes

1 fish or meat stock cube
150 ml (¼ pint) boiling water
125 g (4 oz) tinned flaked tuna in
oil, drained
125 g (4 oz) porridge oats
50 g (2 oz) cornmeal
5 g (¼ oz) fast-action dried yeast
50 g (2 oz) plain flour, plus extra
for kneading
1 small egg, beaten

Fishy feasts

Your dog will find these golden-brown fish biscuit balls irresistible. Serve them as a reward whenever he has been especially well behaved.

1 Dissolve the stock cube in the boiling water and leave to cool.

2 Add the tuna, oats, cornmeal, yeast and flour to the stock and work into a dough.

3 Scatter about 2 handfuls of flour on your work surface, turn out the dough and knead it until all the flour has been worked in. Allow the dough to rest for 10 minutes.

4 Lightly roll out the dough then cut it into 2.5 cm (1 inch) pieces. Shape each piece into a ball by gently rolling it between your palms, dusting them with flour to stop the dough from sticking. Transfer the balls to a nonstick baking sheet and brush with beaten egg.

5 Bake in a preheated oven, 200°C (400°F), Gas Mark 6, for 20 minutes until golden-brown. Leave to cool and then store in an airtight tin.

Makes about 12 chunks
Preparation time 5 minutes,
plus freezing

½ ripe banana or other favourite
fruit, mashed
4 drops of vanilla extract
250 ml (8 fl oz) low-fat
natural yogurt
wafer cone, to serve (optional)

Doganettos

Remember to serve these little treats at room temperature. Even on very hot days your dog will probably prefer to lick the chunks until they dissolve.

1 Mix together the fruit, vanilla and yogurt.

2 Transfer the mixture to a freezer-proof plastic tub, put on the lid and freeze.

3 Cut the frozen mixture into chunks or serve in a wafer cone.

Makes 8–10 biscuits
Preparation time 15 minutes
Cooking time 40 minutes

125 g (4 oz) plain flour, plus extra
for rolling
25 g (1 oz) cornmeal
2 tablespoons dried mint
3 tablespoons dried parsley
50 ml (2 fl oz) water
6 tablespoons vegetable oil
sunflower seeds

Kennel kiss cookies

You could use shaped biscuit cutters for these little cookies, and if you make them smaller than about 5 cm (2 inches) across they won't take so long to cook. Check from time to time to ensure that they don't burn in the oven.

1 Mix together the flour, cornmeal, dried mint and parsley in a large bowl. Add the water and oil and mix thoroughly to make a dough.

2 Turn out the dough on a lightly floured surface and roll it out to 5 mm (¼ inch) thick. Cut it into shapes with biscuit cutters.

3 Decorate the shapes with sunflower seeds and transfer them to a nonstick baking sheet. Bake in a preheated oven, 180°C (350°F), Gas Mark 4, for 40 minutes until lightly browned.

4 Allow the biscuits to dry out in a warm place (close to a radiator is ideal) for several hours. Store them in an airtight container to keep them crisp.

Crunchy cornflake cakes

Makes 8–10 balls
Preparation time 10 minutes
Cooking time 15–20 minutes

3 tablespoons low-fat sunflower or vegetable spread
50 g (2 oz) demerara sugar
1 small egg, beaten
50 g (2 oz) plain flour
2 handfuls of cornflakes, lightly crushed

These little cakes are definitely not for everyday consumption. Keep them as a special treat for outstandingly good behaviour.

1 Cream together the spread and sugar until light and fluffy.

2 Add the egg and sift in the flour. Stir together quickly to combine.

3 Roll teaspoonfuls of the mixture in the crushed cornflakes, then transfer the balls to a nonstick baking sheet and cook in a preheated oven, 190°C (375°F), Gas Mark 5, for 10–15 minutes. Transfer to a rack and allow to cool.

Bonzer's pitta patty burgers

Serves 1–2
Preparation time 15 minutes
Cooking time about 10 minutes

250 g (8 oz) lean minced beef or lamb
1 egg, beaten
1 tablespoon fresh wholemeal breadcrumbs
2 tablespoons natural yogurt or low-fat cream cheese
2 wholemeal pitta breads

Pitta breads are convenient containers for these little burgers, but they do go soggy if they are left standing around with the filling inside, so fill them at the last minute.

1 Mix together the meat, egg and breadcrumbs. Divide the mixture in half and form it into 2 patties, each about 2 cm (¾ inch) thick. If necessary, lightly flour your hands to stop the mixture sticking to them.

2 Place the patties under a preheated medium-high grill for about 5 minutes, then turn them over and grill for another 4 minutes, or until browned and crisp on the outside and fully cooked inside. Allow to cool.

3 Top each patty with a tablespoon of yogurt or cream cheese and place inside a pitta.

Recipes for celebrations

As a valued member of your family, your dog should be just as much a part of special celebrations as anyone else. These treats are the canine equivalent of caviar and champagne. And remember to make something special for his birthday to make it an unforgettable occasion.

Serves 4–6
Preparation time 10 minutes
Cooking time 30 minutes

175 g (6 oz) self-raising wholemeal flour

50 g (2 oz) demerara sugar

2 tablespoons dried skimmed milk

2 small eggs, beaten

5 tablespoons cold water

small spoonful of sultanas

2 generous tablespoons clear honey

4 generous tablespoons mascarpone cheese

dog chocolates, birthday candles and holders, and dog figurine to decorate

Barker's birthday cake

For an occasion to remember make this delicious cake for your special friend. Don't forget to take a photograph before it's eaten.

1 Put the flour, sugar, milk, eggs, water and sultanas in a large bowl and beat together to make a light, airy mixture.

2 Lightly grease 2 round cake tins, each 18 cm (7 inches) across, and spoon the mixture into the tins. Bake in a preheated oven, 180°C (350°F), Gas Mark 4, for 30 minutes. When they are cooked, a metal skewer inserted into the centre of each cake will come out clean. Transfer to a wire rack to cool.

3 Slice off the top of one cake to level it. Mix together the honey and 3 tablespoons cheese and spread the mixture on the levelled cake. Place the other cake on top and cover it with the remaining cheese.

4 Decorate the cake with dog chocolates and the appropriate number of candles.

Furry pupcakes

Makes 8–10 cakes
Preparation time 15 minutes
Cooking time 35 minutes

2 small eggs, beaten
6 drops vanilla extract
½ ripe banana, mashed
6 tablespoons cold water
125 g (4 oz) self-raising flour
25 g (1 oz) plain wholemeal flour
1 tablespoon demerara sugar
1 tablespoon sunflower seeds
¼ teaspoon cinnamon
1 tablespoon dried skimmed milk
mascarpone cheese and dog
chocolates, to decorate

Don't forget to peel away the paper case from these cupcakes before you offer them to your dog.

1 Cream together the eggs, vanilla, banana and water in a mixing bowl and lightly fold in all the dry ingredients.

2 Line a 12-section muffin tin with paper cases and spoon the mixture into the cases so that they are half full. Bake in a preheated oven, 180°C (350°F), Gas Mark 4, for 35 minutes or until light brown. When they are cooked, a metal skewer inserted into the centre of the cakes will come out clean.

3 Transfer the cakes to a wire rack to cool, then decorate each cake with 1 teaspoon of mascarpone cheese and 2 dog chocolates.

Bow-wow cake

Serves 1–2
Preparation time 15 minutes
Cooking time 2 minutes

10 digestive biscuits
45 g (1½ oz) low-fat sunflower or
vegetable spread
150 g (5 oz) low-fat soft cheese
thin slices of ripe mango, banana,
apple or other fresh fruit,
to decorate

If your dog could choose, this is probably what he would want for himself. Your friends will be pretty impressed by it, too.

1 Put the biscuits in a strong plastic food bag and crush them with a rolling pin.

2 Melt the sunflower or vegetable spread in a saucepan over a low heat. Transfer to a bowl, add the crushed biscuits and combine well.

3 Lightly grease a 15 cm (6 inch) dish and spread the mixture over the base, pressing it down firmly. Cover the biscuit base with the cheese and chill in a refrigerator until set.

4 Decorate the top of the cheesecake with slices of fruit and serve.

The weekly workout

All dogs need to burn off excess energy to prevent weight gain, and if your dog is denied the level of physical and mental activity he needs his energy may be channelled elsewhere – such as chewing his basket or digging up your flowerbeds.

How far and when

Dogs love exercise, but just like humans they can overdo it. Puppies in particular need to exercise little and often in order to built up strength in their joints and muscles, and mature dogs need to achieve fitness over a number of weeks or months. Create a fitness programme that is individually suited to your dog.

WALKING

If you want to find out how much exercise your dog is getting every day you should invest in a Petometer, which counts the number of steps your dog takes and how many calories he is burning. This gadget is useful if your dog needs to burn a few extra calories or if you want to try new forms of exercise together because it allows you to build the amount done daily bit by bit. It's also fun to see how much farther than you your dog walks on an ordinary off-lead walk.

Whether or not you are able to let your dog off his lead will largely depend on whether you have access to a safe area and whether you can get him to come back when you call. If you are able to let your dog off the lead, he will relish the opportunity to follow scents, run, chase toys and play with other dogs. It is not only large breeds, such as Labradors and Boxers, that enjoy a good run, but also smaller breeds, such as Jack Russells and West Highland Terriers.

If you have a hound, such as a Beagle, it is even more important that you can call him back to you, because once he picks up the scent of a rabbit or a fox it can be hard to stop him from following it. Never risk letting your dog off his lead when you are near livestock.

RUNNING

If you enjoy running, why not take your dog with you? As long as your dog is fit, healthy and over 12 months old and as long as you build up the distances gradually, then it is safe for both of you. Dalmatians in particular will enjoy the opportunity for some steady running.

CYCLING

Cycling with your dog can be a great way to enjoy exercise together, provided you build up the time and type of terrain gradually. It's important that your dog does not become overheated as he tries to keep up with you, and remember that smaller dogs – Miniature Schnauzers, for example – will not be able to run as fast as, say, a Golden Retriever. Vary your speed and distances accordingly.

If you decide to cycle holding your dog on a lead, make sure that your dog is trained to run in a straight line, without pulling forwards or backwards, before you venture out on a public road. Gadgets that attach the lead to the bike by means of a spring allow the tension in the lead to be absorbed rather than pulling your bike off course and causing an accident.

How much is too much?

A minimum of 40 minutes twice a day is usually sufficient for most adult dogs, but this will, of course, vary according to the dog's breed, age and fitness and the weather conditions. Dogs need to build fitness levels gradually to avoid straining muscles or harming joints, but as long as they are over 12 months old and are fit and healthy, they can cope with almost any amount of exercise.

Enjoying your outings

For many dogs, walks are the highlights of their day. Sights, sounds and smells stimulate their senses and they will throw themselves into investigating the environment, hunting for prey and engaging in social encounters. There are some simple things you can do to make each walk even more exciting for your dog.

FETCH

A ball is a great toy for the park and will provide your dog with hours of fun. There are many different types of balls available – from soft and squidgy ones to firmer, more hardwearing types. There are even those that squeak. Always make sure that balls are large enough not to be swallowed. Some people find a ball on a rope easier to throw than an ordinary one, and it does mean that there is always a part of the toy you can get hold of when you want to retrieve it. If you don't have a good throwing arm, you can

invest in a special flexible stick to make the ball go that little bit farther.

Alternative toys for outdoor games include frisbees and plaited ropes or raggers. Some dogs love chasing and catching frisbees, while others will run for the frisbee but don't seem to possess the eye–mouth coordination needed to catch it. If you and your dog become really skilled at playing frisbee, there are even competitions you can enter.

If your dog likes a good game of tug, try incorporating it into the walk. Throw a tug toy for your dog to fetch, then when he comes racing back to you with the rope in his mouth you can have a great game of tug before asking him to drop the toy so you can throw it again.

FOOTBALL CRAZY
Most dogs love playing football (soccer), and the game has a great advantage over other ball games because it's impossible for a dog to pick up a football in his mouth. Instead, he will run around chasing it for hours to his heart's content, nudging it along with his nose. Special plastic dog footballs that cannot be burst by even the most enthusiastic of dogs are available from most pet shops. Football is a game for all the family and will keep you fit as well as your dog!

HIDE-AND-SEEK
Many dogs love to play hide-and-seek. When your dog is away from you, simply hide behind the nearest tree (without your dog seeing) and then call him to you. Your dog then has to come and find you. Make some noises to begin with to give your dog a clue to where you are, but once he has got the hang of it, start being quieter so he has to work harder to find you. Always make sure you give your dog lots of praise and rewards for finding you. Playing hide-and-seek in the park will also improve your dog's recall abilities.

Play by the rules

Teach your dog to let go of a toy on one single command by swapping the toy for a small treat such as a piece of cooked meat, cheese or frankfurter. Alternatively, use two identical toys when playing fetch. You keep one in your hand then swap it for the other when your dog returns to you. This method not only encourages your dog to let go of his toy but it will also really get him racing.

TREASURE HUNT

Dogs have an amazing sense of smell, so take advantage of it to play the following game. Without your dog noticing, hide one of his favourite toys or a pot of treats in a small area of the field you are walking in (you may need someone to hold your dog for you while you do this). Return to your dog and ask him to find the hidden article. Make it really exciting for him by giving him lots of encouragement as he tries to sniff out the toy or treats. As soon as he finds it, give him lots of praise and either have a really enthusiastic game with the toy or reward him with treats. Gradually make the game harder by hiding the toy or treats in more difficult places and farther afield.

TRACKING AND SEARCHING

Your dog's natural ability to use his nose can be channelled by taking part in more formal tracking and searching events. In these, a scent is laid for your dog to follow or articles are left along a trail for your dog to find. This is something any breed can do – you don't have to own a Bloodhound – and it is great to watch your dog following an 'invisible' trail and doing something that comes so naturally to him and brings him such enjoyment.

You can arrange a tracking session for yourself or you can join an organized group. If you want to do it yourself, simply lay a track in your garden or a local field. Walk by dragging your feet through the grass rather then stepping, and occasionally drop some tasty treats or a toy, along the way. Your dog will actually follow the scent of crushed vegetation, and finding the rewards will help keep him motivated.

FOLLOW THE LEADER

Encouraging your dog to follow you off-lead is fun for your dog and can also help prevent your dog from pulling while he is on the lead. You can begin by dropping small treats by your side for your dog to eat as you walk along. Progress to holding the food in your hand, giving him a piece every so often. Change direction regularly and vary your speed from a slow walk to a run.

FOOD CIRCUITS

Try combining two aspects of dog heaven: chasing and food. Call your dog to you, and as he comes to you have a small treat in your hand.

Use this to encourage him all the way around your back in a circle, and then throw the titbit away from you for him to chase. Call him back to you again, around your back and throw the treat away from you. As your dog gets better the game will become quicker and you will be able to throw the food farther away from you. This game can also improve your dog's recall by making the action of returning to you part of a game. Herding breeds in particular adore it.

Rewards at the ready

Always make sure you carry some tasty titbits with you when you go out for a walk. You never know when you may want to reward your dog for that super-fast recall. See pages 34–35 for some tasty homemade rewards.

IN WITH THE IN-CROWD

Consider how much you enjoy meeting friends and sharing experiences with them. Our dogs are no different. For the social among them, there is nothing better than meeting up with familiar friends at the local park and chasing and playing together. Such groups often form spontaneously, or over time as owners get to know one another and enjoy company while walking their dogs.

Social groups offer help, friendship and even training practice for dogs and owners who meet up regularly. It is possible to work on behaviour such as recall from play when your dog is socializing with other dogs – a training practice that would otherwise be difficult to set up and control. If you are new to an area and feel that your dog is lacking in canine pals, try consulting the local press or the Internet to find out if there is a local training group you can join.

GROUNDWORK FOR FUN

There are two factors that will make outings with your dog truly pleasurable. The first is his ability to walk well on the lead. Not only will you return home with two arms the same length, but your dog will appear more approachable and well behaved than if he is straining at the lead.

The second is that you are able to let your dog off the lead in safe areas, such as the local park. It is good for dogs to let off energy in this way, but it's only possible if you have trained him to come to you when you call.

Alternatives to walking

Daily exercise is vital for all dogs, but there's no need to do the same old walks every day. There are plenty of alternatives that you can try. If your vet has a noticeboard in the waiting room you may find some advertisements for clubs and groups. Libraries, community centres and local directories are also worth checking out.

AGILITY CLASSES

Joining your local dog agility club is a great way for you to meet new people and for your dog to make new friends. All dogs seem to really enjoy agility classes, and you don't have to take part competitively. Your dog will learn to negotiate jumps, tunnels, hoops and high walks, which is not only great fun for him but is also a good way of improving off-lead control. Any breed can do it, but there should be no jumping before the age of 12 months, while bones and joints are still developing.

Before you join an agility club ask if you can go along to watch a class to make sure you are happy with the training methods that are used. Agility should be fun, not strict or disciplined, and each piece of equipment should be introduced slowly and carefully. The dog should not be forced to do anything he doesn't want to, but gently encouraged in the early stages through the use of food and toy rewards to reinforce good behaviour. If you and your dog get bitten by the bug, there are plenty of competitions you can enter.

Making a mini-obstacle course

You can make a mini-obstacle course in your own garden or backyard.

- Reasonably priced play tunnels for children are available in toy shops, and they are suitable for dogs if they are secured carefully to prevent rolling.

- Make mini-hurdles from bamboo canes balanced on upturned buckets or pots so you can adjust the height for your dog.

- A low-level dog walk can be constructed from a plank of wood balanced on bricks. You can even balance a plank on a single pile of bricks to make a mini-seesaw.

FLYBALL COMPETITIONS

Flyball is a fast and furious game that is based on a relay race. Dogs must run in a straight line away from their owner, jump over four hurdles, trigger a special box to release a tennis ball, catch the ball and then run back over the four hurdles and 'hand over' to the next dog in their team. Any breed or size of dog can take part, because the height of the hurdles is set to be appropriate for the smallest dog in the team. Flyball is now a popular spectator sport, so even if your dog isn't interested, you might find it an entertaining way to spend the evening.

WORKING TRIALS

Working trials were developed to test the working ability of dogs and date back to the 1920s when police dogs competed against each other to demonstrate their skills in tracking, searching, agility and control. Trials are now open to all and although the large working breeds still dominate the events, there are categories for smaller breeds. Dogs learn to track and search for missing objects, negotiate high jumps and long jumps, walk to heel, retrieve a dumb-bell, come when called, stay when told and be sent away from the owner to a particular spot.

Training for this sport requires much practice and often involves being out in all weathers, so it's not for the faint-hearted. However, to watch dogs demonstrating their natural abilities in the field makes all the effort worthwhile – and your dog will love it.

Keep it fun

All these exercises should be thought of as games, and it is important to keep the training light-hearted and fun. The owners who keep the training enjoyable tend to have a lot more success and enjoyment than those who feel they must win at all costs. Dogs are not machines: they respond to encouragement, praise and rewards.

Hydrotherapy is a wonderful alternative to exercise on land. There are now a number of hydrotherapy pools that offer the opportunity to exercise your dog without a referral from your vet due to injury or illness (see page 91). Swimming helps to increase both fitness and stamina and will improve your dog's muscle tone. Not every dog will be keen on getting into the pool at first, but with gradual acclimatization they should soon grow in confidence. Some pools let the owner swim with their dog, which can help in the early stages. Bear in mind that a five-minute swimming session for your dog is reputedly the equivalent of an 8 kilometre (5 mile) walk, and because hydrotherapy can be a vigorous form of exercise, it is worth checking with your vet before the first session to make sure your dog is able to participate safely.

Never force your dog into water if he does not want to go. He should enjoy the games you play together. Don't force him to play these games just because you think they're fun.

DANCING WITH YOUR DOG

Also known as heelwork to music or freestyle, dancing with your dog is great fun. Many dog owners find it hard to teach their dog to walk next to them without pulling on the lead, but as soon as you add music, owners suddenly become a lot more motivated to train their dog to perform clever tricks.

The element of fun makes it much more interesting for your dog too. The variety and different paces and rhythms mean that your dog has to stay alert all the time, so you are providing not only physical exercise but mental stimulation as well. Tricks are often introduced to give more of the 'dance' element. As a sport heelwork to music is becoming more and more popular and recognized, so there are a number of clubs offering lessons to dogs and their owners. If you get really involved in this you may even decide to take part in competitions.

SWIMMING

Some breeds of dog enjoy swimming more than others. If you have a dog that was bred to work in and around water, such as a Newfoundland, Poodle or Labrador, they will especially love to go swimming, but other dogs, from Boxers to Collies, enjoy it too. Some dogs may only enjoy paddling, but others are happy to go out of their depth and swim properly. Make it even more fun by encouraging your dog to retrieve a toy – there are special ones on the market that float.

Take great care that currents in rivers and streams are not so strong that your dog cannot cope. If your dog enjoys swimming in the sea, remember that not all beaches are open to dogs all year round.

Try a dance move

The spin is easy to teach and looks great.

1 With your dog standing in front of you, hold a tasty treat close to his nose for him to smell, then move it back in line with his right shoulder.

2 Encourage your dog to follow the treat by moving it back towards his hip.

3 As your dog turns around in a circle keep the treat just out of his reach.

4 Give him the treat once he has turned full circle. Gradually make the spin faster and faster, and when he has mastered the spin build in the spoken command 'spin'.

On-lead fun

Even if you are unable to let your dog off the lead it does not mean that he has to miss out on all the fun. There are still plenty of exciting and stimulating games you can play with him. Investing in a long-line or an extending lead will give your dog a greater measure of freedom.

SEARCH AND RESCUE

This is a great game and all the family can take part, with your dog safely on lead. One person stays with the dog to hold his lead, while everyone else hides, then the person holding the lead allows the dog to lead him to the hidden family members. Always remember to give your dog lots of encouragement and praise and food rewards for finding the 'hiders'.

NATURAL AGILITY

Walks in wooded areas often present natural obstacles, such as fallen trees and low branches. Rather then avoiding these, turn them into an agility course. Encourage your dog to jump over fallen branches for a food treat, or if there are some trees close together, teach your dog to weave in and out of them. If you come across a large fallen tree, use the trunk as the equivalent

of a dog walk, gently encouraging your dog to walk along the top of it. Urban obstacles can also be used in the same way. Make use of all your surroundings to add an element of fun to your dog's daily routine.

FOLLOWING A SCENT TRAIL

You may need to get up early for this exercise because the best time to start your dog off hunting for a scent trail is before the ground outside has been walked on by other people.

- To begin with, choose an area in a park or field with short grass or low-growing vegetation.
- Tie your dog up or ask someone else to hold on to his lead.
- Put a pole in the ground to act as a marker and as a cue to your dog that the game is about to begin.
- Shuffle your feet next to the pole, place a titbit on the floor right next to it, then set off and walk about 3 metres (10 feet) in a straight line, placing titbits along the way as you go. At the end of the track, you can place your dog's favourite toy or a food 'jackpot'.
- Walk back to the pole along the same path.
- Bring out your dog on a long line or long lead. Encourage him to sniff at the base of the pole to find the treat, then show him with your hand where the next part of the track goes so he can find the food and toys.

Leading the way

To make sure your dog doesn't miss out on the fun, use a long line specially sold for the purpose – 8 metres (25– 26 feet) is perfect – or an extending lead. If you are using an extending lead practise using the brake system and never grab the cord or you could cause yourself an injury.

All dogs can track – it's just a case of getting them to do it when you want them to.

LEAD ETIQUETTE

Avoid shortening your dog's lead when you meet other dogs. This gives him the opportunity to say hello to the other dog naturally, without human interference. Pulling one dog away from another can raise his front paws off the ground, which is an intimidating gesture for the other dog.

Take care that you do not let the lead get too long when there are other people around. Apart from the danger of getting your lead tangled up with the other dog's, you must make sure that you never allow the lead to drag along the ground so that it trips someone up. You would be responsible for any damage or injury so caused.

The over-pampered pooch

As much as we want to pamper our pooch and give him the very best things in life, it is possible to overdo it. In recent times there have been more and more instances of overweight dogs that have not been getting enough exercise. But there is help out there if your dog has been enjoying too much of the good life.

DIET AND EXERCISE

We all know the safest and most effective way to lose weight is to eat sensibly and exercise regularly. The same is true for dogs. If your dog is getting a little rounded, cutting back his food intake or switching to a lower-calorie diet will help. Combine this with regular, gentle exercise, slowly building to a more vigorous regime. See earlier in this chapter for some ideas for fun exercises to do with your dog, and see pages 14–15 for advice on understanding your dog's body language so that you know if he really is enjoying the things you are making him do.

SLIMMING CLUBS

Many veterinary surgeries now organize free slimming clubs. These involve taking your dog to the vet at regular intervals to be weighed. His weight will be taken at your first visit and a target weight set for him based on his breed and height. His weight loss can then be shown on a chart to reveal his progress – ideally, it will show that he is getting closer to his target weight with each visit. The embarrassment of having your dog's weight read out in front of a waiting room full of other people and pets will motivate you to do something about it.

HEALTH SPAS

It's now possible to take your dog to luxury resorts that offer him packages of relaxation and fitness, from massage and hydrotherapy to acupuncture and aromatherapy. There are also residential holidays available, which are aimed at helping both dog and owner in body and mind.

FAT CAMPS

Some specialized camps for overweight dogs have been established in recent times. These look at not only all aspects of your dog's diet but also his exercise regime. The camps aim to train both dog and owner to follow a healthier way of life – training that they will take home with them and carry on together.

Before you undertake any new exercise programme or change your dog's regime in any way you should discuss the changes with your veterinary surgeon. If you are overweight, as well as your dog, it would be advisable to talk to your doctor too.

When it goes too far

There is a huge array of services available to dogs now, but some of them – such as plastic surgery – are clearly more for the owner's benefit than the dog's. Unless there is a medical reason for your dog to have surgery, you should never subject him to such a procedure. No matter how obsessed we may be with our body image, this obsession should not be transferred to our dogs.

The pooch parlour

When we think about pampering our pooch we initially think
about providing delicious food and making sure that he has
a comfortable, warm bed. But looking after the outer dog –
making sure his eyes sparkle and his coat shines – can be
just as important.

Teeth that gleam

Your dog's teeth are his permanent weapons. They are what sets him apart as a top predator, and they deserve to be kept in pristine, gleaming condition. Like humans, dogs suffer from tooth decay and gum disease if their teeth are not kept clean. This can lead to pain, infection and bad breath – and we all know how this can put us off wanting to bestow kisses.

BRUSHING A DOG'S TEETH

Establish a regular dental checking and cleaning regime for your dog. Canine dentistry has come on in leaps and bounds over the last few years, and veterinary medicine links many health problems to poor dental care – so no excuses: get brushing.

If your dog suffers from dental disease it may be necessary for his teeth to be descaled under anaesthetic. The teeth are then polished to create a smooth surface.

All dogs need to be accustomed to having their teeth brushed, and although chicken- or liver-flavoured toothpaste might seem tempting many dogs do not appreciate the actual brushing action and need to be trained to accept it as part of their daily routine. Use specially designed dog toothpaste – not one made for humans – and a dog toothbrush that has been designed to clean all the surfaces of a dog's tooth at once. You can also use a finger brush, which fits on the end of your finger, allowing you to sweep the brush end gently over the teeth. Take special care when you're cleaning the back molars – your dog might bring his jaws together unexpectedly.

Most dogs take some time to adjust to regular tooth brushing, but little and often is the key. A thorough clean should take 10–15 minutes. There are many chews and treats available that claim to keep your dog's teeth clean and his breath fresh. Use these in addition to regular cleaning.

The brushing routine

Follow these simple steps to clean your dog's teeth.

1 Choose a flavour of canine toothpaste that you think your dog will like. Put a little paste – about the size of a pea – on the brush.

2 Lift his lips one side at a time.

3 Work from front to back, sweeping the brush from the gum down to the tooth to dislodge any remaining food and to gently massage the gums.

4 Brush the inner surface of the teeth, praising and rewarding good behaviour.

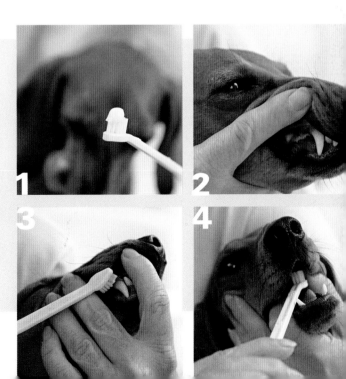

Cleaning ears, eyes and paws

Every time your dog steps out of the front door, he should look and feel his best. A good starting point for any beauty routine is to check that your dog is in the peak of health, and his eyes, ears, mouth and feet will give you essential clues to his level of wellbeing. Make sure he enjoys it by offering plenty of praise and treats.

EAR PROTECTION

The inside of a dog's ear canal should appear as clean, pink skin. Brown deposits or an odd smell may indicate either an ear infection or the presence of ear mites. Some owners like to pluck the hair from their dog's inner ear for cosmetic purposes, but this cannot be recommended. It may cause the dog pain, and it is possible that the hairs protect the inside of the dog's ears from foreign bodies, such as grass seeds, which might otherwise get lodged there and cause irritation, or even infection.

Never push anything into your dog's ear – cotton buds, for example – because these can damage the eardrum. Deeper wax or a smelly discharge may indicate that medical treatment is necessary, so ask your vet for advice.

If you have a dog with pendulous ears, such as a Cocker Spaniel or a Basset Hound, you should pay additional attention. Being so long these types of ear are more prone to collecting grass seeds and becoming infected, so they will need to be checked on a regular basis.

1 **To clean your dog's ears, lift his ear flap away from the head and peer down into the ear canal to check for any obstruction, brown wax or infection.**

2 **Working gently, use cotton wool, dampened with water or saline solution, to remove any dirt on the earflap or outer parts. Use a different piece of cotton wool for each ear to avoid cross-infection.**

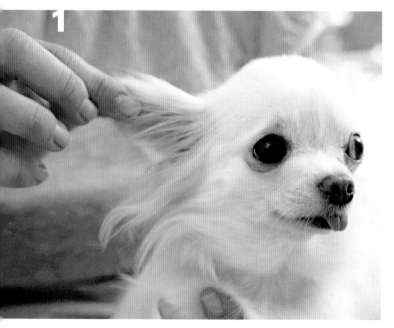

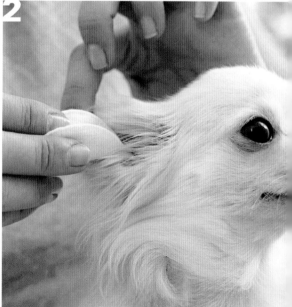

EYES FRONT

Your dog's eyes should be clear and bright, sparkling with health and mischief. Any cloudiness, permanent changes in the pupil size or redness should be assessed promptly by the vet.

Like humans, dogs can also suffer from conjunctivitis. This needs treatment from your vet but is usually cured relatively easily. Light sensitivity, a weeping eye or any attempt by the dog to rub at his eyes with his paws may indicate a foreign body in the eye, which is likely to need urgent veterinary attention.

Some dogs' eyes have a tendency to weep, causing a brown stain to develop underneath, which, while not indicating ill health, certainly prevents them from looking their best. This condition seems to affect Poodles, Chihuahuas and Bichon Frisées in particular. Gently wiping the dog's face with damp cotton wool (see above) may help, and special tear-stain removal products are available from your vet or pet store.

GLAMOUR PAWS

Teaching your dog to stand still while you check his feet is essential, and should be done with patience and through rewards and kindness. The pads on the bottom of a dog's paws are generally quite robust but, like humans, dogs can suffer from blisters and cuts if they have been over-exerting themselves.

Use scissors to trim the hair between the pads of paws in longhaired breeds to avoid matting (see below). This is particularly important in summer to prevent grass seeds from lodging between the pads and in winter, in snowy weather, to prevent the dog from gathering snowballs on his feet.

Making your dog's coat shine – bathing

How often you will need to bathe your dog will depend on the breed, whether or not you show him and the individual dog's behaviour. Some dogs seem to deliberately wait until the day after their bath to go and roll in something smelly – perhaps it's the canine equivalent of applying Chanel No. 5!

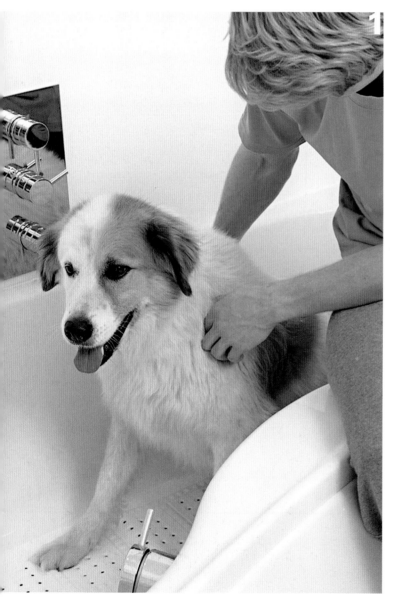

BE PREPARED

It is important that you gather together all the equipment you will need before you start, because having to run off halfway through a bathing session to grab the shampoo or towels will lead to chaos. Not many dogs will simply stand still if they are left alone in the bathroom soaking wet.

You will need:
- Bath or sink or, if outside, a large container and water supply
- Non-slip rubber mat
- Dog shampoo – choose an appropriate one for your dog's coat type, colour or breed
- Dog coat conditioner
- Dog towels
- Brush and comb
- Hairdryer
- Supply of treats

1 Lift your dog into the bath, sink or container and give him a couple of minutes to become accustomed to his surroundings. Putting a rubber mat underneath him before you begin will make it less slippery and give your dog more confidence. Reward him and praise him with treats for calm behaviour.

2 Soak the dog all over with tepid (not hot) water, using a shower attachment or a jug. This needs to be thorough, because it will affect how effective the shampoo will be.

3 Dilute the shampoo, which makes it easier to distribute, and lather it as you go, paying particular attention to grubby areas. Many dogs enjoy a massage at this stage and this will also increase the cleansing action of the shampoo.

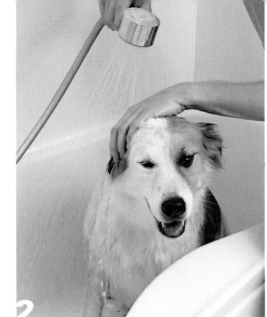

4 Rinse well with clean water, then rinse again. Make sure that the water runs clear and that all the shampoo has been completely removed. This is important to prevent flaky skin and itchiness. Massage in a dog conditioner. There are some great brands available made with natural products. Keep your massage strokes slow and calming. Rinse thoroughly, again until the water runs clear.

5 Finally, wrap your dog tightly in a towel and lift him out of the bath. Towel dry to remove as much moisture as possible, then brush and comb your dog and either allow him to dry naturally or use a hairdryer.

Tip

Dogs tend to shake themselves when their heads are wet, so to avoid a soaking yourself, leave his head until last when wetting and shampooing. Do not allow your dog to dry naturally outdoors in cold weather because he might catch a chill.

Making your dog's coat shine – grooming

Grooming your dog regularly is one of the most cost-efficient ways of pampering him. Time is all you need to spend. Don't leave it to the professionals; get those brushes out and give it a go. Your dog will really appreciate the close contact he has with you during your grooming sessions.

ROUTINE GROOMING

Grooming sessions should always be fun, so make sure that you schedule them for a time when both you and your dog are feeling relaxed. Until your dog is used to being groomed, keep the session short – just 5–10 minutes – but gradually lengthen the time until it becomes part of your routine. Pile on the praise and offer your pooch his favourite treats. He'll learn to love it.

How often you groom your dog and the equipment you use will depend on his coat.

SMOOTH-COATED BREEDS

If you have a dog with a smooth, short coat – a Boxer or Pug, for example – you can adopt a low-maintenance regime.

Use a rubber brush to loosen dead skin, dirt and loose hair, and then polish your pooch with a chamois cloth until he shines.

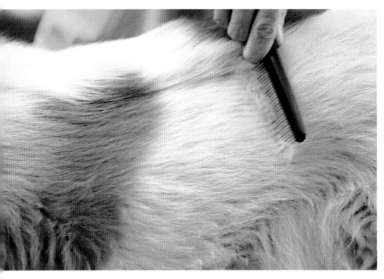

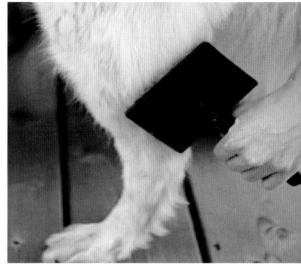

WIRE-HAIRED BREEDS

Dogs such as Schnauzers have harsh, dense coats that give them a distinctive appearance. They are relatively easy to maintain with weekly grooming and professional trimming or stripping.

Begin by brushing against the grain of the hair, then brush going with the grain. The outer wiry coat becomes soft when it is too long and should be removed, either by clipping or by hand stripping.

CURLY-COATED BREEDS

Dogs such as Poodles and Portuguese Water Dogs were originally bred to live and work around water. Their thick, tight, curly coats trap air, insulating the dog from water and cold air. Regular grooming that includes clipping is essential to keep the coat looking its best.

Daily at-home grooming with a steel brush is essential for curly-coated breeds, and you should follow this with a wire slicker to remove dead hair and control tangles.

DOUBLE-COATED BREEDS

Many popular breeds, including the Golden Retriever and German Shepherd Dog, have a double coat. A soft undercoat serves as a protective barrier against the elements. The outer coats come in a variety of lengths and textures, from the straight and harsh, such as the Pomeranian, to the long and silky, such as the Afghan Hound and Yorkshire Terrier.

Regular grooming with a slicker brush (see above, right) will help remove dead hair and debris from the inner and outer coats. Work on the undercoat with a wide-toothed comb (see above, left), paying particular attention to areas that are prone to matting, such as behind the ears, the mane and the legs. Finish with a chamois cloth to make the coat gleam.

Special occasions

We all like to look good for special occasions, and so do our dogs. Spray conditioners are available that will give your dog's coat extra shine. And why should it just be Bichon Frisées who get the best cuts? Many breeds can be clipped (see pages 70–73). Will you be attending a wedding accompanied by your Poodle this year? There are now dog-friendly hair-dyes – pink is the most popular colour for the big day.

Nail trimming and polishing

Why not treat your dog to a pedicure? It can be done quite easily at home if you know how. Some dogs need their nails trimmed more often than others. Some breeds don't need to have their nails trimmed at all, but that doesn't mean they have to miss out. You can still file and buff them, or even apply nail polish!

FEET FIRST

If you have never cut your dog's nails before, make sure you get him used to having his feet handled before you start out. Reward him with treats and plenty of praise for allowing you to handle him. Follow these simple steps to trim and polish your dog's nails:

1 **Find a position that is comfortable for both you and your dog. For small dogs this could be on your lap or a raised surface; for larger dogs the floor will be more convenient. Relax your dog with some soft music and a gentle massage before you start (see pages 77–85). Then, using an ordinary nail file, clean the dirt from under your dog's nails.**

Nail polish

On very special occasions you might consider applying some nail polish. Do not use human polish. Instead, apply an epoxy enamel polish available for dogs from grooming suppliers. There are some fabulous colours available, which you can choose to coordinate with your own favourite outfits.

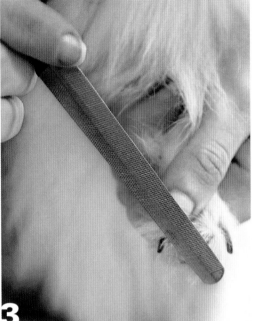

2 Locate the 'quick'. This is the pink part of the nail that has a blood supply to it. Do not cut this part of the nail – it will hurt. In dogs with white claws it is easy to see the pink quick. In dogs with black claws it is more difficult, so it is advisable to cut only the very tip off so you do not run the risk of cutting the quick. (If you do accidentally cut the quick it will bleed. Either apply a coagulant product or press firmly on the end of the nail until the bleeding stops. If you are in any doubt seek veterinary advice.) Cut only the tip of each claw – about 1 millimetre (1/25 inch) is usually sufficient – working from underneath, not from the top downwards. Ensure a smooth cut by gently squeezing the clippers. Cut quickly and cleanly, and do not be tempted to pull down to break the tip off – it will fall away when you cut through.

3 File any sharp edges away with a file – many dogs enjoy this part of the process.

4 Finally, use an ordinary nail buffer to polish the nail. Continue with the rest of the nails on that paw and make sure you regularly reward your dog with words, petting and treats. Move on and repeat for each paw.

Dew claws

Dew claws are located on the inner side of the paw, the equivalent of the human wrist. They are usually found on the front paws only, but some breeds, such as Pyrenean Mountain Dogs and Beaucerons, have them on the back paws as well. Not all dogs have dew claws because some breeders remove them on puppies. These nails do not touch the ground, so they cannot wear down naturally. Check them regularly and clip them to keep them short.

The latest cuts for the modern mutt

Stroll down any street in Beverly Hills, New York, London or Paris and you are sure to see a dazzling array of preened pooches sporting all manner of fabulous and freaky hairstyles. From primped Poodles to dainty Dandie Dinmonts, modern dogs are all about style. Eye-catching hairstyles are not exclusively the preserve of 21st-century dogs, however, and if you search as far back as the Renaissance you will find some stylish canine curls, perfected by aristocratic dog owners. Here are a few suggestions for some of the best styles for the dog about town. For closely-cropped cuts, take your dog – with a photograph of the style you like – to your regular grooming parlour.

LION'S MANE

Any breed with a decent volume of curly hair – Poodles, Portuguese Water Dogs (see left) Labradoodles and Schnoodles, for example – can pull this off. It is fairly practical style: the short coat is easy to groom and is perfect for summer, while the mane just looks fabulous.

Simply trim the main body of the coat to a summer length, leaving enough hair to work with around the neck and shoulders. Build up a thick, opulent mane by blow-drying and back-combing the remaining thick hair.

The style doesn't require a huge amount of maintenance to keep it looking great. Trim the main coat every fortnight to make sure that the 'mane' remains prominent.

LUSCIOUS LOCKS

For those pooches with long, flowing locks, such as the Yorkshire Terrier, Afghan Hound, Briard or Old English Sheepdog, maintenance is very important to prevent matting.

To help keep the coat silky and smooth, and to enable it to grow, curl papers are ideal. The dog's hair is separated into equal-sized sections

and each lock is carefully rolled up with a curl paper and secured with a rubber band. This will keep the hair out of the way and clean. Often the dog's hair is kept in papers at all times and they are only removed for the show ring.

If you want your dog to be able to run free with his buddies in the park but do not want to go to the trouble of using curl papers, another option is the 'puppy cut'. The coat is trimmed short and evenly all over, giving your dog that cute fluffy puppy look.

PUNK'D

If you have a breed with medium-length hair, such as a Poodle or a Pekingese, you might want to try this low-maintenance style. When you are clipping back the fur for the summer, leave a Mohawk on top of the head and watch the reactions. It looks best with a studded collar. This style occurs naturally in the hairless Chinese Crested Dog (see top right).

SKATER DOG

Dogs with tightly curled coats, such as Poodles, Labradoodles, Schnoodles, Portuguese Water

Dogs and Schnauzers, will look stunning with this practical style. Most breeds with tight curls were bred to work in water, and the fur was often left long over the knees and elbows to protect the joints and major organs. Today it is a traditional style for show dogs.

Clip the body of the coat, leaving pompons covering the knees, elbows and hip joints (see below). This is a low-maintenance style, which needs only a fortnightly trim to keep it tidy.

BRAIDED BEAUTY

This funky style, which is suitable for Poodles and other medium- to long-haired dogs, is surprisingly easy to achieve and the results are very effective (see above). Separate the hair into equal-sized sections and use small coloured elastic bands, beads or lengths of cotton to tie the hair at regular intervals. It's easy to do and is a great look for a night on the town.

THE TWISTED SISTER

This high-maintenance style (see top right), which resembles a colourful skater dog (see page 71), is suitable for Poodles, Portuguese Water Dogs and Curly Coated Retrievers. It involves using a dye on the head, body and the pompon parts of the knees and elbows.

This is not an easy style and requires a professional groomer. You must make sure that any dyes you use are safe for dogs and pay particular attention to clipping and keeping the hair tidy.

RASTA PARTY

If you have a Komondor or Bergamasco you will find that this look styles itself (see right).

Wash and condition the lengthiest parts of the coat and sit back and watch the natural dreads emerge. It's an easy style to achieve because the dreadlocks are natural. It works well in summer and is useful if the fur is too short for a proper trim but slightly too long to keep neat and tidy.

SUPERBANGS

When you are clipping the outer coat of longhaired breeds, especially Yorkshire Terriers, Afghan Hounds, Irish Setters and Old English Sheepdogs, leave the hair on the top of the head long and encourage it to fall forwards, perhaps with a bow or ribbon. Most of these breeds are used to their fur covering their eyes, so this is a natural style for them (see above).

This style needs little more than a quick trim once a month to maintain it.

THE CANINE MULLET

Take your longhaired dog, especially Afghan Hounds, to the groomer and ask for a normal clip but to leave the back long. Remember to comb through the long bits for that 'business up front, party at the back' look (see top right).

This is a superb style for dogs that work in water because it enables them to keep their back legs warm and their front legs neat and tidy.

THE POIROT

If you have a Schnauzer, Bearded Collie, Irish Wolfhound, Irish Terrier, Russian Black Terrier or Griffon Bruxellois take the long fur around the dog's mouth and muzzle and twist it into an eye-catching handle-bar moustache (see below). This requires no products or equipment, just your hands, and not only will it make your dog look as if he could solve crimes but it will also keep food out of his fur when he is eating.

The New Age hound

Some complementary therapies that we take for granted as part of
our own health and beauty routines can also be applied to our dogs.
Massage is probably the most important of these, but there are
several techniques, including aromatherapy and relaxation therapies,
that you should add to your armoury of pooch-pampering practices.

Aromatherapy for dogs

The word 'aromatherapy' was first used in 1937 by the French cosmetic scientist René-Maurice Gattefosse, who discovered that the volatile extracts distilled from some aromatic plants had a profound effect on the skin. He accidentally burned his hand and treated the wound with neat lavender essence, which immediately eased the pain. The wound healed well, with no sign of infection and not even a scar to remind him of the accident.

Essential oils are highly concentrated substances extracted from the leaves, stems or flowers of aromatic plants. The oils are usually captured by a method of steam distillation.

Buy essential oils from a health shop and make sure the bottle is labelled '100 per cent pure essential oil'. The oils vary in price, because some oils, such as lavender, are easily extracted from plentiful plants, while others, such as rose, are extremely expensive because it is so difficult to extract oil from the flowers. There are plenty of wonderful oils available at reasonable prices, and these are therapeutic for your pet and a pleasure to use.

ESSENTIAL OILS AND YOUR DOG

Because essential oils have antiseptic properties, it is a good idea to add a few drops to the rinsing water when you are wiping down dog beds and toys.

Ticks, which can be a problem for your dog, are picked up in long grass. A drop or two of eucalyptus essential oil applied directly on to the body of the tick will cause it to drop off. This is the only purpose for which you should use neat essential oil on your dog.

Aromatherapy burners will scent your room, providing a calm or uplifting environment and effectively banishing dog odours. Put some water in the top of the burner and add 4 drops of your selected essential oil. If you light a tea candle or night light in the space beneath, you will experience the wonderful scents from your chosen oils for several hours. If you do not wish to use candles for safety reasons, add the oils to a small bowl of hot water. The scent will fade as the water cools.

ESSENTIAL OILS AND DOG MASSAGE

Although aromatherapy oils can be used in many ways with your dog, massage is one of the most popular. You will require a base or carrier oil, such as grapeseed or olive oil, although you can use more expensive oils, such as jojoba or almond oil. Base oils are available in small quantities from health shops. Use 1 teaspoon of base oil to 1 drop of your chosen essential oil and mix them in a small container.

Place a little oil in the palm of your hand and rub your hands together. When your hands are coated in oil, gently run them through your dog's coat, adopting a slow, rhythmic stroking motion. Always avoid the face. The result is a wonderful relaxing treatment for your dog that conditions his coat at the same time. If your dog is not happy with the scent you have selected you can try another, but it is a good idea to massage with the plain, unscented base oil first and once he is used to the idea introduce a more strongly scented essential oil.

You can also buy natural aromatherapy dog products, including shampoos, conditioners and coat mists, which contain pure essential oils in therapeutic blends.

Some of the most widely used essential oils and their uses are listed in the table on page 76.

Guide to essential oils

Oils	Characteristics and use	Application
Camomile	Expensive; soothing and calming for dry skin	Massage or burner
Cedarwood	Sweet woody scents with antiseptic benefits	Massage or burner
Cinnamon	Strongly scented so use sparingly	Burner
Clary sage	Deodorant benefits with calming effects	Massage or burner
Eucalyptus	Insect repellent (good against ticks); antiseptic and stimulating properties	Massage or burner
Geranium	Balancing oil, with calming and soothing effect	Massage or burner
Grapefruit	Fresh, uplifting aroma with antiseptic properties	Burner
Lavender	Inexpensive; wonderful all-round oil	Massage or burner
Lemongrass	Fresh, uplifting aroma with antiseptic properties	Burner
Peppermint	Uplifting and antiseptic; use sparingly	Massage or burner
Rosemary	Uplifting oil with fresh scents; good for skincare and dandruff	Massage or burner
Ylang ylang	Floral oil with calming qualities	Massage or burner

Essential oils should not be used to treat any skin conditions your dog may be suffering from and should never be used if your dog's skin is broken. If you are in any doubt, it is advisable to consult your regular veterinary surgeon or a holistic veterinary surgeon.

Because dogs have a far superior sense of smell to humans, it's important to be extra careful about the scents and ingredients that you use. Rosemary, cinnamon, coriander, lavender, basil and orange are all popular in the canine aromatherapy industry, and you can even buy aromatherapy kits for dogs. Some of these include gadgets that make it possible to fix scented items to your dog's collar so that he can feel the benefits all day long.

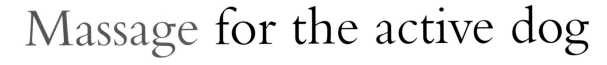

Massage for the active dog

Massage was used by the ancient Greeks and Romans to enhance their general health and fitness and specifically to improve muscular function and endurance. Centuries ago animals also benefited from the therapy. Dogs practise self-massage by licking themselves, even when they have no obvious injury.

HOW MASSAGE WORKS

Massage works at many different levels on the body's systems, and the use of different techniques can effect huge changes within them. Therefore it is extremely important to understand how massage will affect your dog's body as a whole.

The most important principle for applying massage to your dog is 'to do no harm', and before you undertake any massage techniques you should look at the guidelines for when massage is not appropriate summarized on page 79.

Massage influences the circulatory system (the flow of blood around the body). This system consists of two types of blood vessel: arteries and veins. The arteries carry oxygenated blood from the lungs and the heart around the body, and they also carry nutrients from the intestines. They deliver these vital components to every single cell in our bodies. Each cell is equivalent to a 'mini-body', so it has to eat, drink, respire

Note

If you are in any doubt about your dog's health and condition and whether massage is appropriate for him, seek veterinary advice.

and excrete. The veins operate as the waste-collection system, which acts through the lungs, from where carbon dioxide is expelled from the body and through the kidneys and liver. The oxygen-depleted blood is returned to the heart and lungs where it is re-oxygenated before starting its journey around the body again.

The immune or lymphatic system is separate from the circulatory system but works alongside it. It acts as a secondary waste-disposal mechanism, picking up the larger fragments of waste left by the veins, including any bacteria or viruses contracted from outside the body.

WHEN TO MASSAGE

Applying massage before a walk results in the increased flow of blood to the muscles that the dog needs for walking and running. This, in turn, creates more warmth and enhanced elasticity of the muscle fibres, which helps the muscles to operate more efficiently and can prevent minor muscular injury. Massage therapy also provides an instant guide to your dog's health. By passing your hands over the animal's entire body you can feel excessive warmth or lumps, allowing an early opportunity for a diagnosis by your vet.

When you apply massage after a walk it helps to cleanse your dog's muscles of waste by again enhancing blood flow. The waste products that can accumulate in the body cause stiffness, which is often evident when a dog gets up after lying down for a while.

> ### Warning
>
> The Veterinary Surgeons Act 1966 and the Exemption Order 1962 make it illegal in Britain and the USA, respectively, for anyone to practise massage on any dog other than their own.

Pre-walk benefits

A pre-walk massage will...

- Enhance the blood flow to muscles for improved health
- Warm the muscles to help prevent injury
- Give you the opportunity for a hands-on health check of your dog
- Provide an enjoyable bonding experience between you and your dog

Post-walk benefits

A post-walk massage will...

- Enhance the blood flow thereby helping to remove waste products
- Stimulate the dog's lymphatic system to further cleanse his body
- Ease stiffness by encouraging waste removal
- Give a hands-on health check
- Provide an enjoyable bonding experience between you and your dog

EFFLEURAGE

Effleurage is a stroking technique, and is used for both the pre- and post-walk massages. It is applied by the palm of the hand, fingers and fingertips. It is done by applying an even pressure throughout, and in this it is similar to a deliberate stroke. The best way of judging if you have the correct technique is by your dog's reaction: if you are successful he will probably lean into you in enjoyment of the process.

Keep your hands and wrists relaxed while you massage, gently gliding over the surface of the dog's coat. Be especially careful to use less pressure over his joints.

When you are applying the massage use one hand with the pressure of a deliberate stroke, (less is more), and keep the other hand gently and reassuringly on another part of your dog. This is extremely important for physical support and continuity of stroke. Massage with the lie of the coat, not against the main coat (see right). The only time we massage against the coat is up the back of the legs in a post-walk massage.

PRE-MASSAGE PREPARATION

The pre-walk massage is most easily practised when your dog is standing. The post-walk massage can be applied with your dog standing or lying down.

Make sure your dog is comfortable and well supported on a secure surface, preferably the floor and not a table or raised object. It is best if he is in a familiar environment that is free from distractions such as food, toys and playmates.

Before you start to massage always show your intention by using a special word or phrase like 'Warm up' or 'Warm down' in a light, friendly manner or by making any connection with your dog that indicates your intention.

WHEN NOT TO MASSAGE

Massage works on every level in the dog, and it can affect your dog physiologically (the way his body functions) and psychologically (how he functions emotionally). It's therefore important to be certain that it is safe to massage your much-loved pet.

Massage your dog only when he is well and healthy, because if you massage when he is ill, you could interrupt the body's natural self-healing process and prolong the illness.

Do not massage your dog if he does not want you to. If you find any tender areas in the course of a massage seek immediate veterinary advice. Massage can have a negative effect on diseases such as cancer and heart conditions. Check with your vet if you have doubts about your dog's health or suitability for massage.

Warning

If you are driving before you go for a walk, do not let your dog jump out of the car as this can cause muscular injury.

Contraindications

Do not massage...

- If your dog is ill or has a fever

- If your dog has a skin infection; never massage over a lump or open wound, over a recent fracture or over the site of an injury or recent operation

- If your dog has a heart condition

- If your dog has cancer

- If your dog is still panting excessively after a walk

- If your dog is in clinical shock

- Immediately before or after food

- If your dog is dehydrated

- If your dog does not want a massage

The pre-walk massage

This is an excellent way to get your dog's mind and body ready for the exercise that is essential for his health and vitality. It will help prevent soft tissue injury and promote muscular and joint health. It could also benefit your dog's muscular balance and positively reflect within his muscles and joint health in later life.

The whole pre-walk routine should take no more than 5 minutes. The massage must be fairly brisk but not rough – about 60 strokes a minute – and can be given up to 20 minutes before exercise. When you are both newcomers to massage begin slowly until you feel confident of the process. Apply each stroke three times over each different area, keeping your hand relaxed and following the contours of your dog's body. Be alert to your dog's reactions so that you can gauge your touch.

Remember, massage is a partnership and a bond-enhancing technique; it is not something to be inflicted on your dog.

1 Start with your hand behind your dog's ear, at the top of the neck. With a stroking motion, follow the neck down in front of the shoulder and finish on your dog's chest between his front legs. Repeat three times.

2 Continue at the top of the dog's shoulder, massage down, stopping at his elbow. Repeat three times.

3 Place your hand back on the top of the dog's shoulder, this time with your fingers facing his tail. Gently massage from the shoulder all the way down the dog's back either side of his spine. (It is important to avoid applying massage directly over the dog's spine.) Repeat three times.

4 Continue the move described in step 3 all the way down to the tail.

5 Pointing your fingers downwards, massage gently down the front of the hind leg, finishing at the knee. Repeat three times.

6 Keeping your hand and fingers pointing in the same direction, massage your dog's 'engine' muscles, the powerful muscles at the top of his hind legs. Repeat three times. Repeat the routine on the other side of your dog's body.

The post-walk massage

After a long or active walk, lactic acid can develop and remain within the dog's muscles; this can cause stiffness after rest. These symptoms will ease, but if the acid remains within the muscles it will cause micro-damage to the fibres. This cleansing massage can help to alleviate the symptoms of lactic acid build-up.

After strenuous exercise your dog will benefit hugely from a post-walk massage. This should not be carried out immediately after the walk. First, you must let your dog relax and allow any signs of exhaustion or extreme thirst to pass. When the dog is back to a relaxed condition, you can give him a post-walk massage anything up to 4 hours after the exercise.

This massage will help avoid both short- and long-term discomfort from muscular stiffness, which can have detrimental effects on joints in later life. The massage assists in the removal of waste products from the dog's muscles by way of the veins and lymphatic system (see page 78). It must be much slower than the pre-walk massage – 15–20 strokes a minute – to aid relaxation. Be gentler so that you do not aggravate an existing or new injury.

Use the same preparation as with the pre-walk massage, making sure that your dog is secure, safe and preferably dry. Using the same effleurage stroke techniques used before the walk, repeat each stroke three times. This time the dog can be in a lying position. As with the pre-walk technique, indicate your intention to massage before you begin.

As you work, take special care to feel for any excessive heat over joints or muscles. If such symptoms exist consult your vet.

1 Start with your hand behind your dog's ear, at the top of the neck. With a stroking motion, follow the neck down in front of the shoulder and finish on his chest between his front legs. Repeat three times.

2 Move to the top of the dog's shoulder and massage down, stopping at his elbow. Repeat three times.

3 Next, gently massage down the front of the foreleg to the paw. Repeat three times.

4 From your dog's front paw, move your hand around to the back of his foot and massage up the back of the leg to the elbow. Repeat three times.

5 Place your hand on top of the dog's shoulder with your fingers facing his tail. Massage from the shoulder all the way down his back either side of the spine, as in the pre-walk routine, but this time stop at the groin. (It is important to avoid applying massage directly over the dog's spine.) Repeat three times. Finally, massage down the back and front of the dog's hind legs as before but stopping at the knee. Repeat three times. Repeat the routine on the other side of your dog's body.

Relaxation techniques

Many of the relaxation techniques we use ourselves are also appropriate for our dogs. We all need time to wind down and forget the stresses of the day. If your dog has had a hectic day – chasing next door's cat, meeting friends in the park, travelling to the grooming parlour – give him plenty of time to become de-stressed.

EXERCISE

This is a superb way of preventing the need for more hands-on relaxation techniques to calm your dog down later in the day. A well-exercised dog is more likely to be relaxed when he is indoors. Try some of the exercises described on pages 47–57, such as frisbee throwing, football, tug games and flyball. Even a good wrestle can burn off energy. If you have a retrieving breed, such as a Labrador, he will love to fetch balls and would probably do so for as long as you were prepared to throw them. If you have a sight hound, such as a Greyhound, you will be surprised how much fun and exercise he can have chasing the beam of a torch or a shadow. Larger, guardian breeds, such as Pyrenean Mountain Dogs, may just enjoy a gentle stroll.

One of the best ways to ensure that your dog is properly exercised is to play sniff-and-seek games. Canine hide-and-seek might not sound like a serious proposition, but it actually stimulates integral areas of many dogs' natural instincts, such as scent tracking. People that are lost in avalanches are only too glad that the St Bernard who finds them likes a good game of hide-and-seek, and now you can bond with your dog indoors or outdoors with this fun, obedience-oriented and stimulating activity (see page 49).

Start your dog off by carrying a strong-smelling, high-value treat – such as a biscuit or chew – with you when you go to hide. When he finds you, reward him with the treat and issue lots of praise.

DEEP BREATHING

By getting into your dog's space, whether that is on the floor or on the sofa, you can pass on the benefits of deep breathing exercises by doing them yourself.

Hold your dog close to you; if he is a big dog it might be easier just to lie close together. Begin by taking in large breaths and holding them in for three seconds each. Of course, your dog won't be able to copy what you do, but he will be able to feel the calmness that you are resonating in your personal space.

JACUZZI

If you're lucky enough to have a spa bath or Jacuzzi, don't be selfish – let your dog in every now and then to enjoy the relaxing sensations of the bubbles against his skin. Some dogs love having baths and some love swimming, so there is no reason why your dog won't enjoy hopping in with you next time you have a relaxing soak in the Jacuzzi. The benefits of water therapy such as this are numerous. Older dogs with mobility and joint problems will find great relief in the weightless sensation of being in the water and

will benefit from the therapeutic effects that the warm jets of water can have. Dogs with injuries also reap the benefits as the soothing effects of the Jacuzzi may help reduce the swelling on any knocks or bumps they may have picked up.

Be sure to supervise your dog at all times when he is in the Jacuzzi, make sure the water is not too hot for him before he enters, and don't let him spend more than 10 minutes in the water at any one time. Finally, make sure you clean out hairs from the filters afterwards!

YOGA

Yoga for canines – also known as 'doga' or 'ruff yoga' – has become increasingly popular in recent times. Dog yoga is based on the same principles as human yoga – but without the leotards! In fact, dogs have been practising yoga for thousands of years: you may have noticed your dog stretching when he wakes up in the morning or after an afternoon nap; the popular yoga position *adho mukha svanasana*, or 'downward-facing dog', is derived from this type of canine stretch.

Dog yoga is proven to soothe even the most stressed-out of pooches. The idea is that you guide your dog gently through various yogic shapes and stretches, helping to improve his circulation and the mobility of his joints, and to reduce the aches and pains associated with over-exertion or old age. You may find, at the end of a session, that your dog's breathing is in synch with your own. At the same time yoga brings you into physical contact with your dog, something that is known to improve the emotional bond between the two of you and to bring about improvements in your relationship.

Don't attempt to perform yoga with your dog without professional supervision. Look out for classes in your area that you can attend.

REFLEXOLOGY

This is the practice of using various techniques to apply pressure to the reflex points on the feet or hands. These reflex points are believed to be connected to other areas in the body and stimulating them sends electrical pulses to these areas. Reflexology treatment has recently been made available for dogs. When a dog is ill or exhausted, the passageways between the reflex points and their corresponding areas can become blocked. Stimulating the reflex points on a dog's paw can help to release the blockage and return the flow of energy to normal, thereby restoring your dog to health.

Remember, many dogs have sensitive areas on their feet, so begin any treatment slowly and stop at once if your dog indicates that he is not enjoying the sensation.

DEEP RELAXATION

Unlike humans, dogs cannot be hypnotized into a state of deep relaxation. However, you can use techniques similar to hypnotism to help calm your dog. Why not try sitting with him either on your lap or by your side in a dimly lit room with some soothing music in the background and, using only the power of your voice, attempt to persuade him into a state of utter relaxation?

Holistic therapy

Holistic therapy has become popular among humans lately, but it is only relatively recently that it has been used for dogs. Conventional medicine is by no means inferior to holistic remedies, but sometimes alternative methods of treating canine ailments prove to be more effective.

Holistic therapy focuses on the whole of the body, rather than the area of the body that is directly presenting symptoms of ill health. This approach widens the areas that are likely to be treated – for example, skin problems could be tackled with a nutritional solution and emotional problems could be tackled with a physical approach.

HYDROTHERAPY

This offers a therapeutic, relaxed and enjoyable workout, which can otherwise be difficult for dogs suffering from arthritic joints or following injury or surgery. Controlled swimming allows the muscles to be stimulated and exercised without the stress that is associated with land-based exercise, which can often cause pain to an ill or injured dog.

Vets often recommend to owners a course of hydrotherapy for pre- and post-surgical conditioning, to reduce weight in obese animals, for the painless exercise of pets with arthritis or dysplasia, for cardiovascular workout for seniors, as rehabilitation for stroke sufferers and for pain management. It is, therefore, of use in the case of many orthopaedic conditions both pre-operatively to improve muscle tone of affected limbs – for example, before total hip replacement – and post-operatively in conditions such as cruciate ligament rupture, osteochondrosis or fracture repair, when light swimming can begin as soon as the sutures have been removed.

Hydrotherapy techniques help to relieve pain and strengthen and re-train muscles because the dog is effectively weightless while he is swimming. It works by encouraging a full range of joint motion, thereby improving muscle tone without imposing undue stress on damaged tissues. This is why results can occur so quickly.

ACUPUNCTURE

This is a non-painful procedure to stimulate healing and pain relief without drugs, and it is used extensively in many veterinary practices, especially to treat muscle and bone pains. Many dogs have benefited from the gentle healing effects of acupuncture, and the process is becoming increasingly popular.

Acupuncture has been used in the East for thousands of years. The Traditional Chinese method talks of energy, *qi* (pronounced 'chee'), which flows around the body in meridians, or channels. Trauma, excessive heat, cold and damp can disrupt the flow of *qi*, and this stagnation leads to disease in the relevant joint or organ. The needles for which acupuncture is famed stimulate *qi*, restoring the normal flow to maintain healthy joints and organs.

The practice involves placing short, ultra-fine needles in specific areas that are known as acupuncture points. These are small points on the skin that have a good nerve supply, and stimulating the area with needles causes reflex impulses to move up to the spinal cord to change the operation of pain receptors in the spine. Signals are sent to the brain and back to the affected area to affect inflammation and pain perception and to promote healing. Acupuncture should never be attempted by an amateur.

Dogs suffering from rheumatism, arthritis and skin conditions may have their symptoms treated with acupuncture. The onset of age-related problems such as bladder weakness can be slowed if acupuncture is a regular part of your dog's routine. Visit your vet to find out more.

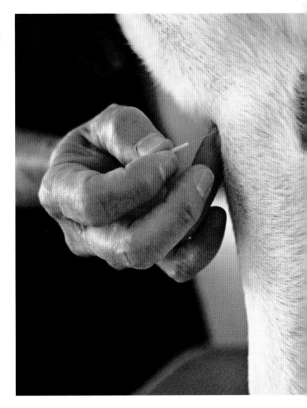

the all-natural complete foods that are available commercially. Some of the ingredients rich in essential nutrients and that are used in many all-natural pet foods are described below.

BROWN RICE

Brown rice, which is renowned for its health-promoting properties, is the natural state of rice with just the husk removed (see bottom left). It contains calcium, iron, some zinc and the B vitamins thiamine, niacin and riboflavin. In Chinese medicine brown rice is utilized for its cooling effect on the body, and it is believed to be able to regulate the spleen and stomach, to clear heat and to provide energy.

CHICKEN

Chicken is a highly digestible source of protein, so small amounts can satisfy the nutritional needs of most dogs. It is believed to have a warming effect on the body, enriching *qi* (energy) and the blood, while toning the kidneys. Chicken oil is a good source of omega 3 fatty acids. Holistic vets work on the principle that meat should be used to treat like with like, and chicken liver is given to nourish the liver.

OATS

This whole food (see below) has antiseptic properties and is supposed to help prevent the contraction of contagious infections.

NUTRITION

All the nutrients needed for a balanced diet at every stage of your dog's life are available in a non-processed form. Be prepared to do your research and spend a lot of time preparing your dog's meals if you are thinking of feeding only natural ingredients in their raw form. The recipes on pages 34–45 use a range of natural ingredients, and you can experiment with flavours and textures that your dog particularly likes. Alternatively, consider feeding him one of

SEAWEED

Nutrient-rich sea vegetables contain vitamins A, C, D, E, B1 and B2, as well as phosphorus, potassium, calcium, iron, iodine, fibre, sodium and small amounts of protein. Most importantly, the iodine in seaweed supports the function of the thyroid, which controls the body's metabolism, especially protein metabolism.

SUNFLOWER OIL

This low-cholesterol oil (see right), which is high in polyunsaturated fat, is also naturally rich in vitamin E.

NATURAL REMEDIES

Holistic vets use a wide range of plant-based remedies to treat the dogs in their care. These remedies should be given to your dog only under the guidance of a qualified practitioner.

- **Garlic** (See left.) As well as being good for keeping the heart healthy, garlic is useful for treating fleas because it makes the taste of the blood intolerable to them.
- **Greenleaf** This useful herb helps a number of health problems, including eczema. It can also be used to relieve stiffness and arthritis.
- **Parsley** A member of the carrot family, parsley is rich in iron, vitamins C and A, calcium, potassium and phosphorus and is a great supplement for overall wellbeing.
- **Skullcap** This is a good remedy if your dog suffers from travel sickness or anxiety. It is also useful in treating the symptoms of epilepsy, although it is certainly not a cure for it.
- **Tea tree oil** This is a fantastic antiseptic and anti-inflammatory treatment for sprains and strains (see left).

Reiki and Tellington Touch™

As we move further into the 21st century, the more we seem to look into the past for innovative yet traditional methods of healing our bodies and those of our dogs. Eastern medicine and healing practices are becoming increasingly popular, and reiki and the Tellington Touch™ are both natural, non-medicinal practices that have been shown to benefit the body and mind, not just for us but for our dogs too.

REIKI

Even though they have been domesticated for some 15,000 years, dogs retain many of their natural instincts and fears. This means that some dogs experience difficulties in adjusting to the modern, human world that they inhabit. Reiki is one method of relaxing and settling a dog that may be suffering from fear or anxiety or acting aggressively. It is also an effective healing method for physical ailments.

Reiki is a Japanese form of healing, and the word is a Japanese translation of a Chinese word, which is said to mean 'energy' or 'soul'. It is said that reiki is an intelligent energy, which, when it is conducted though the body of your dog, will know where to go and what ailments to heal.

During a reiki session the dog will lie down while the practitioner will act as the conductor for the energy. The practitioner channels the energy around the dog's body with his hands, concentrating on the spine as a central avenue for the energy to travel.

The physical benefits of the treatment are said to include increased vitality, improved immunity and reduced blood pressure for dogs with high blood pressure. Emotional and mental benefits include reduced anxiety, greater focus in training and higher levels of alertness.

TELLINGTON TOUCH™

The Tellington Touch™, or T Touch™, is a method
of healing and adjustment intended to accelerate
convalescence from illness or injury, to eliminate
undesirable behaviour patterns and to strengthen
the bond between a dog and his owner.

Tellington Touch™ is based on the circular
movement of the fingers and hands across the
entire body, and the practice is designed to
stimulate increased cell function in the body.
Each circular touch is complete within itself.
It is not necessary for the practitioner to have
wide anatomical knowledge, but it is important
for them to seek advice about performing the
procedure before they carry it out on a pet, so
make sure that any practitioner you approach
has experience of working on dogs.

The Tellington Touch™ technique was
developed by internationally recognized animal
expert Linda Tellington-Jones and is based on
cooperation and respect between animal and
human or human and human. One of the main
benefits of the therapy is that a rapport is
developed between the practitioner and the
recipient of the procedure. If your dog is
uncomfortable when he is being handled,
Tellington Touch™ is one method of removing
the natural fear responses that he may
experience when humans try to touch him.
Consequently, the animal may become more
responsive to being taught new and more
appropriate behaviours.

As with any healing practice, discontinue if
your dog shows any sign of discomfort.

The puppy inside

Keeping your dog in top condition means looking after every aspect of his appearance. Many modern human beauty treatments can be adapted to pamper your dog, and while you're attending to his outer needs, don't forget to keep his mind healthy by devising some special games to keep him occupied.

Beauty therapies

Beauty therapy is no longer the preserve of the rich and famous, and facials and hair treatments are no longer exclusive to humans. Pampered pooches have got in on the act, and now the most picky Pomeranians and spoiled spaniels around are demanding five-star luxury treatments for their face and fur. These are not all the kind of treatments you will want to do at home – some of them are quite messy – but ask your grooming parlour if they can carry them out for you.

FOAMY FACE WASH

This is a treatment you can apply yourself. Choose from the many canine face washes that are available, including citrus scented, minty and even specially formulated moisturizing washes. Rinse the fur on the face with warm water using a flannel or sponge. Apply a small amount of face wash solution and lather in. Take great care around the eyes, even if the preparation claims to be sensitive. Rinse out the foam after about a minute and towel dry.

BENEFITS

Many of the face washes specifically designed for dogs will improve the condition of the fur as well as cleaning it. The fur of longhaired breeds, such as Yorkshire Terriers and Cocker Spaniels, can get matted, and conditioning face washes are excellent for alleviating the problem.

MUD BATH

Mud baths that are designed as luxury skin and fur treatments don't use just any old kind of mud. The fresh mud, which is readily available in health and beauty shops, is enriched with other ingredients, including various aquatic plants. It is heated and gently applied to your dog's coat – if it's the first time it may be better to apply the mud to small sections so that your dog can get used to the process. The mud is left to dry for up to an hour, then gently brushed from the fur. The skin is then rinsed with warm water.

BENEFITS

One of the main benefits of this treatment is increased blood flow, which in turn rejuvenates and improves the condition of the skin. The coat should look healthy and clean after a mud bath. Older dogs often enjoy improved mobility because the warmth from the mud bath can aid joint locomotion and general recovery.

SEAWEED WRAP

This is a cooling and exfoliating algae mask that covers your dog's entire body, without restricting it too much. First, your dog's coat will be cleaned

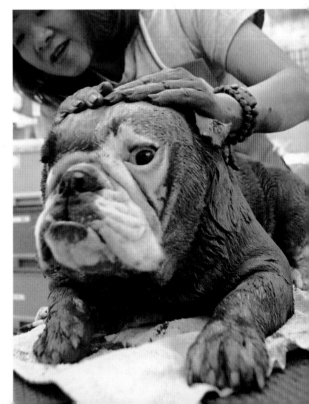

then exfoliated with a seaweed gel. Finally, the warm seaweed wrap will be applied.

BENEFITS

One benefit is exfoliation, which is good for dogs that are suffering from dry, flaky skin, eczema, psoriasis or even the after-affects of fleas. The treatment also remineralizes the skin and fur, leaving the coat looking and feeling healthy. The seaweed contains many purifying and enriching minerals, which are excellent for leaving your dog feeling rejuvenated. The coat should be left looking glossy and healthy, ideally with a pleasant residual smell that should last until your dog takes his next dip in a pond.

MEDICINAL WATER BATH

If you have some spare money and a large bath this could be the most luxurious and beneficial treat you could give your dog. Mineralized medicinal baths are an exceptionally effective natural rejuvenation remedy. Thermal spas and springs are excellent sources for this sort of treatment, but preparations for home use can be bought in health shops and online.

BENEFITS

The main benefit to be derived from a warm medicinal bath is the relaxation for the dog. Old dogs in particular can gain enormous benefit from this sort of treatment because the minerals in the bath can help with rheumatism and arthritis. The dog's coat will benefit too from being soaked in the water.

INTENSIVE CONDITIONING

Whether your pet has a curly mop, flowing locks or a retro crop, he is almost certain to sustain a certain amount of damage to his coat through his natural dog-like activities, such as rolling in mud and dragging himself through bushes. Intensive conditioning, which you can do at home, returns essential oils to the fur, which provide that healthy, glossy look that will make your dog stand

in the crowd. Use a proprietary product and apply it to the entire coat or to sections.

BENEFITS
An intensive conditioning treatment will moisturize dry fur, nourish damaged hair and revitalize a tired coat. The conditioner will not only remove dirt and grime from the base of the coat, but it will also improve the look of your dog and help protect against fleas and ticks.

ROSEMARY HOT OIL TREATMENT
This is a healthy and invigorating solution to unhealthy or damaged fur. Put a handful of rosemary leaves and half a cup of olive oil in a small saucepan and warm them gently over a low heat. Massage this into the fur, wrap your dog in a warm towel and leave for up to 15 minutes. Remove the towel and rinse away the oil with warm water.

BENEFITS
This treatment is ideal for dogs with dry or damaged fur. The nutrients in the oil solution nourish and replenish the natural moisture in the fur, leaving the coat looking and feeling much healthier.

SCALP MASSAGE
This is similar to the traditional intensive massage, but it pays special attention to the head, ears and neck of the dog. Either visit a professional or seek advice on how to perform this technique yourself.

BENEFITS
An intensive scalp massage will improve your dog's circulation and relaxation, and if you learn to do it yourself it can benefit your relationship with your dog too, as you will be able to spend some special time with him.

DENTAL TREATMENT

As with humans, a dog's teeth may become damaged and unhealthy as life goes on. There are several excellent canine teeth treatments, including non-foaming, meat-flavoured toothpastes, which can be applied with special brushes (see page 61). One of the easiest ways to look after your dog's teeth is to supply him with plenty of chews, so that the friction on his teeth helps to clean away any bits of food. Make sure that you supervise your dog while he is chewing rawhide bones and take away any smaller pieces that he has chewed off the bone to minimize the risks of choking and intestinal blockage.

BENEFITS

Having healthy teeth and gums is essential to your dog's overall health. Bad teeth mean that dogs cannot eat and digest their food properly, which can lead to weight loss. There is also the possibility of abscesses in the mouth, which can lead to poisoning.

FEED THE FUR

Feeding the fur is about feeding your dog foods that will benefit his coat. Sprinkling linseed oil on his food is one way of supplementing his diet to get great results, but increasing the amount of fish, such as salmon and tuna, in his diet will also dramatically improve the condition of his coat.

BENEFITS

A healthy, glossy coat is the sign of a healthy, happy dog. Replacing some of the meat in your dog's diet with fish can also promote weight loss, and increase joint mobility in older dogs.

NEEM LEAF BODY WRAP

Neem leaves are used in some cultures to kill parasites. The leaf has therapeutic properties and is used in some luxury skin care products.

BENEFITS

A neem leaf wrap nourishes the skin and removes blemishes and irritations. It eliminates parasites and leaves the skin moisturised and refreshed.

Brain games to play indoors

Too often dogs are left to their own devices for large parts of the day, and it is not surprising that a bored dog develops bad habits, such as basket chewing. However, if you keep your dog's mind as active as his body, you will soon notice the difference in his behaviour.

Dogs not only enjoy mental stimulation – they positively demand it. Nearly all breeds of dog have an identifiable original purpose – whether it be herding, retrieving or chasing rats – and they are prewired to try to fulfil this role. Allowing your dog to use and develop his problem-solving abilities by devising games for him to play indoors will increase his brain power in other areas of life, improving training,

basic obedience and even social skills. It will also allow your dog to act like a real dog. There can be no doubt that mental stimulation is tiring for your dog, and knowing that you are leaving a mentally and physically tired dog alone in the house when you go to work or head out for the evening will be less stressful for you because you won't have to worry about what the house will look like when you get home.

INDOOR TUG GAMES

A good tug game with your dog is always great fun. Choose a suitable toy, such as a knotted rope or a ball on a rope, in an appropriate size. The only rules with this game are that you should always keep the toy low to the ground (so you do not encourage your dog to jump up) and that you should be able to get the toy back from your dog safely and easily. This is the easy bit. During a really good game of tugging, place a tasty treat on the end of your dog's nose and he will happily drop the toy to eat the treat. You can then go back to playing again.

HUNT THE TOY

This is a fun and easy game to play indoors. Hide your dog's favourite toy or put a tasty titbit inside a hollow toy somewhere in the house. Make the searches easy to begin with and make sure you are encouraging at all times. As soon as your dog finds the hidden article, praise him and give a food reward or have a game. Gradually the hiding places can become harder and harder.

You can even progress to a single special 'item' to hunt for, then swap it for a titbit. If your dog gets good at this game, you might even be able to give up hunting for your car keys when you are in a rush.

INDOOR HIDE-AND-SEEK

Dogs love this game, whether they play it indoors or outside (see page 49). Unless you know your dog will stay put in one room until you call him from another, you will need two people. While one of you holds the dog, the other goes off to hide in another part of the house. Start simply by hiding in a different room, but as you play more often make the game harder by hiding in more difficult places, such as behind the bed or in the wardrobe. Always be really enthusiastic when your dog finds you. Finally, while he is busy finding one person, the other person, who was originally holding him, can hide and call the dog. He will end up running from room to room trying to find you both.

Keeping your dog alert

Games and puzzles provide fun and entertainment, keeping your dog mentally occupied and stimulating his problem-solving abilities. Here are a few ideas – a combination of commercially available toys and household items – to start you off. As with all activities, do not force your dog to do anything he doesn't want to.

KING KONG

The Kong is the proprietary name of a hard rubber dog toy that can be stuffed with various food treats. The hole through which the food is placed is quite small, so your dog has to work hard at chewing and licking the toy to get all the food out.

The Kong's shape makes it bounce off in various directions when the dog drops it, which makes it an exciting toy anyway, but once it is stuffed with food it becomes irresistible. Try different combinations of food inside to see whether it has an effect on your dog's level of interest or the time it takes him to empty it. Stuffed Kongs can even be put in the freezer to create your dog's own lollipops, which are great for hot summer days. You can find plenty of ideas for recipes on the Internet, but favourites include cheese spread, peanut butter and mashed banana and yogurt.

BUSTER CUBES AND ACTIVITY BALLS

Both these are food-dispensing toys that your dog can play with by himself when you are out of the house. They can be filled with dry food, and your dog has to move the toy around the floor to get the food to drop out.

You can make your own versions of these toys from empty plastic drinking bottles, which can be filled with food and made to work in the same way. However, play with these should always be supervised, just in case your dog decides to take the direct route to the food and chew through the bottle.

SCATTERING FOOD

Rather than simply placing your dog's food in a bowl and putting it in front of him, why not try encouraging him to work for it? If you feed your dog a dry food, scatter it on the lawn or even, if you don't mind the mess, through the house. It will keep your dog amused for some time while he searches for all the pieces. His enthusiasm and tail wagging will increase as he gets better at the game.

Check it out

Hooked on puzzles? There are now online IQ tests you can do with your dog. Have a look at them to see how bright he really is.

If you usually give your dog a wet food, you can still play a version of the game. Divide the meal in to as many small portions as you can and hide them in dishes around the house and garden.

CHASE THE TREAT

This is a version of the well-known street game chase the lady. With your dog watching, put his favourite toy or treat under one of three boxes or plastic cups. Shuffle the cups around and ask your dog to choose which cup the toy or treat is under. Your dog will have to use his nose to sniff each cup in turn and signal to you which cup is the correct one. This could be by pawing at it, touching it with his nose or simply knocking the cup flying to uncover the treat himself.

Tricks to teach

Training your dog to do a few simple tricks gives you an opportunity to spend real time bonding and having fun with him. You don't have to be a professional dog trainer to teach a dog tricks, and here are a few ideas to get you going. Remember to encourage your dog with praise and reward him with tasty treats.

GIVE A PAW AND HIGH FIVE

These are easy tricks for your dog to start with, because many dogs naturally offer their paw.

1 Make sure your dog is sitting comfortably and give him a tiny piece of food from your hand. Then hold another piece in a clenched fist on the floor. Your dog will initially sniff and lick at your hand, then try using a paw to get to the food. As soon as he does this, say 'Good' and release the treat. Repeat this several times. Now raise your hand off the floor slightly, encouraging your dog to raise his paw higher to reach your hand. Say 'Good' and reward him every time he touches your hand, then add a command, such as 'Paw', just before he offers you his raised paw.

2 Once you have mastered this you can move on a stage to 'High five'. Move your hand slightly away from your dog, so he has to wave his paw in the air. Your dog will soon offer higher and higher paw reaches.

BE A BEAR

Make sure your dog has strong hips and a good sense of balance before you try this game. Breeds with large posteriors find it especially easy.

1 With your dog sitting, hold a food treat a little way above his head. Even if only one paw comes off the floor as he tries to stretch up to reach the treat, say 'Good' and reward him with it. Repeat this a few times.

2 Do the same thing again, but now wait until both front feet come off the floor. Say 'Good' and reward. Repeat.

3 Gradually wait for your dog to offer more height. Give him time and confidence in keeping his balance. Let him rest his front paws on your knee if he needs to at first. Finally, add a command, such as 'Be a bear'.

RIGHT ON TARGET

Teaching your dog to touch something with his nose, on command, can lead to a multitude of tricks – from closing doors to turning light switches on and off. This is called target training.

1 You will need a 'target', such as the lid of an empty margarine tub. When presented with a new object, most dogs will sniff it. As soon as he does this, say 'Good' and reward him. Repeat this, making the target disappear and reappear each time from behind your back. Practise until he is confident.

2 Now stick the target to a door, floor or any other object you want him to touch. Encourage your dog to touch the target and reward him with a treat every time. Gradually reduce the size of the target until you no longer need it. Finally, add a command, such as 'Touch'.

Keeping your friendship fresh

Your dog will be your companion and friend for many years, and you'll probably get into a comfortable routine together of walks, grooming and feeding. However, your family circumstances may change over the years, and it's important that you don't forget your dog when this happens.

NEW BABIES

A new baby in the house will mean that you and your partner will be spending less time with your dog. This is inevitable, but remember that your dog won't understand what's going on and might feel jealous and unhappy.

The presence of a new baby doesn't have to be to the dog's detriment, however. While the baby is asleep during the day, set aside time to spend playing games with your dog or teaching him new tricks, and remember to take him on family walks, with your baby in the pram.

When the baby becomes a toddler, make sure that your dog has a space where he can have peace and quiet to relax, so that he is not continually pestered. The two will soon become the best of friends, but remember whose toys are whose to avoid any arguments.

A NEW PUPPY

As your dog gets older and perhaps a little set in his ways, you might be tempted to get another dog – even a puppy – in the belief that this will give him a new lease of life.

Think carefully before you do this. Consider making your dog more alert by trying some of the puzzles and games outlined on pages 102–105, and remember to play with your dog as you used to do. After all, it's not just your dog that's getting older.

If you do decide to get a puppy, be sensitive to the older dog's needs. Make sure the puppy doesn't constantly pester him, and don't punish the older dog if he gets impatient with the puppy for being mischievous. Make sure you still take the older dog for walks on his own so that he has some time alone with you. And it's important for the puppy to be walked on his own, too, otherwise he will never learn to stand on his own four paws! Remember to make sure your dog feels as loved and cherished as he did when he first arrived in your home.

A NEW ROUTINE

Do you always take your dog on the same walk to the same park at the same time of day? Even though you are exercising your dog every day, he is probably as bored with this monotonous routine as you are.

Have you thought about taking a day trip? Your dog would probably love to accompany you to the local garden centre, the beach or to a forest or some woodland. Try and make the effort to go somewhere new every week. Alternatively, think about trying one of our suggestions for new games, such as agility training, working trials or flyball (see pages 52–55). You will benefit as much as your dog from a new interest and from the possibility of making new friends.

The dog about town

The well-dressed dog will have the appropriate clothes and accessories for every occasion and for every season. Make sure that your best friend is the best-turned out dog on the block with the smartest collar and lead and the most up-to-date gadgets.

Clothes for summer walks

You will want your dog's summer wardrobe to include some of the great designs now available. We all want to look our best, even more so on those warm summer days when we are out and about more. If you have been invited out to a party or want to make a real entrance at a dog show make sure your dog can join in the fun.

T-SHIRT COOL

A stylish dog T-shirt will make sure your dog looks his best in the sun. There are some fabulous designs available, ranging from round-necked to polo shirts. Whether they are plain or patterned or have lettering on the back, it's hard not to look good in a T-shirt. So that there can be no danger that you will meet another pooch with the same T-shirt as yours, try customizing your own with a choice of colours or words to suit your own dog's style.

T-shirts not only look great, they have many other uses too. They can help to prevent scratching caused by itchy conditions, help to protect body wounds after operations and are good for elderly or poorly dogs to wear indoors too keep warm. They also keep thin-coated dogs warm and help show coats to stay clean.

SUMMER SHOWERS

It is a fact of life that it will rain, even in the summer. Protect your dog from summer showers with a lightweight raincoat. These are easy to carry with you on days out, just in case the weather changes.

GET AHEAD

We all know the importance of keeping our head covered on a sunny day, and your dog need not miss out either. There are plenty of dog hats available, from the practical to the stylish, ranging from baseball caps, to more feminine designs. Just make sure that your dog approves of the idea of wearing a hat before splashing out.

SUN CREAM

As well as protecting his head with a hat, make sure that your dog is fully protected while he is out in the sun by applying some sun cream. The cream, which is designed especially for dogs, is non-greasy and easily absorbed. Some brands are available as creams, while others are sprays, which can be easier to apply. If you have a dog with barely pigmented areas of skin it is a good idea to apply a protective barrier to protect against the risk of skin cancer and heat rashes. Some breeds, particularly the Hairless Chinese Crested, are more likely to suffer the effects of the sun than others.

Clothes for autumn and winter walks

The chilly days of autumn and winter need careful thought when it comes to fashion. Warmth and comfort need to be combined with practicality and durability. All dogs, apart from rare hairless breeds, have their own coats, but some dogs, such as short-coated breeds, need a little help to keep warm.

JUMPERS

There can be nothing nicer than to snuggle up in a warm woollen jumper on a cold day. There are many dog jumpers available, with just about every design imaginable, so you will always be able to find one you like, and if you enjoy knitting you will be able to create styles and colours that are certain to make your dog stand out in the park. Make sure you choose a fabric that can be easily washed.

HOODIES

These fashionable tops are a practical and stylish way of protecting sensitive dogs with thin coats from cold winds. They can be padded or fleece-lined, and the hood is detachable on some styles.

His choice

Although many dogs appreciate the extra protection a coat affords in cold, wet weather, do make sure that your dog does not get too hot or uncomfortable in his outfit. After all, we want him to look his best, but he should always feel his best as well. If your dog has a thick coat, be cautious with jumpers or coats: over-heating can cause serious health problems.

ALL-IN-ONE TROUSER SUITS

Dogs that enjoy walking even in the depths of winter may need a little protection, and an all-in-one suit provides the perfect combination of practicality and style. Make sure you get one that is suitable for the sex of your pet.

HATS AND SCARVES

No winter outfit is complete without a matching hat and scarf set, although not all dogs will appreciate wearing a scarf: it does look rather like an unusual chewing toy.

COATS

As with jumpers, it is possible to knit or stitch a style that suits your dog. If you prefer to buy there are some pretty winter coats for female pooches, and you could always buy a male dog a fashionable parka. Fleeces, available in a range of sizes and styles, always look good and will keep your dog cosy. Because they stretch with body movements, parkas are supremely comfortable and are also water resistant. Some coats have detachable sleeves so they can be worn as body warmers, making them last longer then just one season. Waxed jackets are a must for the country hound and they are completely waterproof, stylish and easily cleaned. In fact, they are perfect for even the most macho of dogs!

Warning

With all items of doggy clothing it is important that you check regularly to make sure that your dog is comfortable. If he shows any resistance to wearing an item or displays signs of distress, remove the item immediately.

Accessories to show you care

If you want to show your dog how much you care, make sure that he looks his very best when he is out and about by kitting him out with accessories to suit his outfit. As you look into the subject, you will soon come to realize that there is so much more that you will want for your dog that you didn't even realize he needed.

JEWELLERY

For the ultimate in pampering you might want to buy some special jewellery for your dog. A necklace can complete an outfit, and there are designs, from pearls and diamonds to simpler chains, to suit every pocket. All are beautiful, and some are truly extravagant. For that extra-special occasion you could even complete the look with a matching tiara.

CLIPS AND BOWS

Dogs with longer hair sometimes need to keep it off of their face and out of their eyes. You will find a great range of hair clips and bows on the market that are suitable for dogs, from the classic to the outrageous. For everyday wear a bow may be all your dog needs, but for a special occasion there are some beautiful charm clips available, some encrusted with crystals.

TAGS

In some countries it is a legal requirement for a dog to carry a tag on his collar to identify him and his owner. However, these identity tags can be much more then a simple disc. Make sure your dog will always find his way home with an attractively designed tag to attach to his collar. There are all sorts on offer, in all different shapes, colours and sizes – even ones that flash in the dark! They can really help to complement your choice of collar (see pages 118–121).

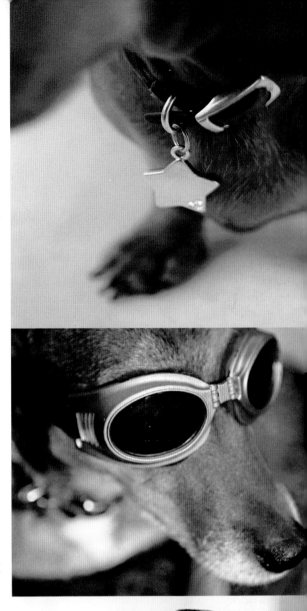

DOGGLES

Dog sunglasses not only look seriously cool but are practical, too. Designed originally for sled dogs to protect their eyes from snow blindness, these canine shades offer protection from ultraviolet light on sunny days. If your dog likes to stick his head out of the car window while you speed along, doggles will protect his eyes from flying grit and debris. They are also great for dogs with eye disorders such as pannus and light sensitivity. Doggles are shatterproof and have padded, anti-fog lenses, and the straps are adjustable for a really good fit. Don't forget to buy a specially formulated doggle lens cleaner to keep them sparkling.

SHOES AND BOOTS

There are shoes to match every dog outfit, including casual trainers and smart boots. Fur-lined boots will keep your dog's feet warm and dry on frosty mornings and a sturdy design will protect his paws from pieces of broken glass.

Think carefully before you encase your dog's feet, however. If your dog has injured a paw it is sensible to protect it while it heals, and a stylish boot may be just the thing he needs. Similarly, if you walk your dog regularly along city streets that use large quantities of salt to prevent ice from forming you might need to cover your dog's paws. In general, however, only breeds with thin coats and exceptionally sensitive skin really need this level of protection.

Gadgets and gizmos

Even if you think your dog has everything a dog could need, think again. There are now some really funky gadgets and gizmos available to make life easier and more fun for both you and your canine friend. In fact, there's no such thing as 'enough' when it comes to your favourite pooch.

designers have thought of everything and include pockets in which you can store dog accessories. The best models have vent holes, and some include a safety collar attachment to help avoid any 'falling' accidents. Some designs are even approved for airlines if you are planning a longer journey.

OVERNIGHT VISITS

When you are staying away from home with your dog on a short break, make sure he can enjoy all the comforts of home with his own personal travel bag. You can either pack your own separate bag or buy one that will contain everything you may need, including non-spill travel water bowls, food-tin lids, treats and thank-you cards. For the ultimate in travelling comfort, a dog sleeping bag will help keep your pooch feeling safe, snug and warm when he's away from home.

BOWLS

You might think a bowl is just a bowl, even if there are some fantastically designed ones on the market. However, just think how handy it would be if you had a self-filling dog bowl, which automatically dispensed a pre-determined quantity of dried food at specific times during the day. This would certainly make life easier for you, and your dog would simply love you for it. Self-filling dog bowls shouldn't be used as a replacement for your dog's regular feeding routine, but they can help if you're unexpectedly away from home for the day and can't take him out with you.

PET CARRIERS

There is a huge variety of pet carriers available to make sure your pooch doesn't get too tired when you are out and about together or for keeping him safe when you travel on a train or bus. They range from simple, sturdy designs to ones made from top-quality leather. Some

WATER, WATER EVERYWHERE

Whether you are in the home or out and about it is vital that your dog has access to fresh, clean drinking water. There is a wide range of dog water fountains available, so pamper your pooch with the luxury of free-flowing, fresh, cool water every day. It will be like having a mountain stream in your own kitchen.

When you are out with your dog, you can make sure that he has plenty to drink at all times with a travel water bowl or a drink-from bottle. Travel water bowls are made of lightweight plastic or nylon, and are very handy if you have access to a water source to fill them. The advantage of the drink-from bottle is that the water can be carried with you and drunk straight from the bottle from a specially designed outlet. Larger dogs could even carry their own water supplies in a dog backpack that is adapted to provide water through a tube either directly to the dog's mouth or into a bowl.

EATING ON THE RUN

When you're out and about with your dog, whether it be on an all-day walk in the country or visiting a friend, nothing could be more handy than a compact, foldaway travel bowl. These are available in all shapes and sizes and can be used for both food and water.

EASY UP

Dog ramps overcome the problem of your having to lift ageing, unwell or arthritic dogs in and out of your car, up on to a favourite chair or other places they might experience difficulty in reaching unaided. The dog simply walks up or down the ramp without assistance – meaning you don't run the risk of developing a back problem yourself.

WIN THE JACKPOT

None of us likes to leave our dog home alone for too long, but when you have to go away you can make sure that he is happy and occupied with his own Kong dispenser (see right). Simply stuff four Kongs with some tasty treats, Kong paste or your dog's own favourite food and place them in the dispenser. At set intervals over a period of four to eight hours, the machine will sound a brief alarm and dispense a Kong for your dog to enjoy. The machine can be mounted on the wall or placed on a counter so the Kong drops to the floor, but make sure that it is well out of your dog's reach in case he cannot wait for the next Kong to come to him and decides to try to empty the dispenser by himself.

Collars and leads to dazzle

Collars and leads used to be functional objects, something you kept in a drawer in the kitchen and pulled out almost as an afterthought as you headed off for the morning walk. Now a visit to a pet store will reveal an astonishing range, and the daily outing will become an opportunity to impress as well as exercise.

PRACTICAL STYLES FOR HER

Of course, there will be times when you want something a little more frivolous for your dog than an everyday collar for a walk in a muddy field, and you may wish to have an array of collars so that you can choose something appropriate for every occasion.

If you have a female dog there are plenty of styles available, made of nylon, leather or canvas, and all in a range of pretty colours and patterns. You could have a collar in every colour of the rainbow, from the softest of pastel shades to vibrant, bold patterns. And, of course, there are leads to match, so you have something suitable whether you are popping out for the morning newspaper or going out for a smart lunch.

For the occasions when style is more important than practicality, you could invest in an ornately decorated collar. There are some stunning designs available, adorned with diamante, crystals, pearls, and even handmade silk flowers, sometimes mounted on velvet. Of course, these are not for everyday wear, but they do look absolutely amazing.

Perfect fit

A collar should fit your dog perfectly for comfort and safety. If it's too loose it might slip it over his head; if it's too tight it will hurt him. You should be able to fit two fingers under the collar when it is fastened.

PRACTICAL STYLES FOR HIM

The range of styles and materials for male dogs is almost as huge as it is for female dogs. There are some fantastic collars in leather, moc croc and canvas. These are often simpler in design than the equivalents for female dogs, but they are practical and stylish and can reflect your dog's personality and the activities he enjoys – denim for cowboys and bikers, for example, camouflage for those who like active pursuits and tweed for country-lovers. Don't forget the matching lead.

You might prefer to eschew anything too fancy for special occasions – a simple but stylish look is what you're after. Some leather collars have simple stitching detail enlivened by a diamante buckle and bone-shaped pendant. Moc croc collars with a subtle diamante design look good on any furry neck, and if your dog really wants luxury, patent leather and rhinestone accents should keep him happy.

SIZE MATTERS

A small dog or puppy needs a collar and lead in a lightweight material that is strong yet comfortable. An over-sized release clasp is useful for easier fastening and unfastening.

Choose a wider, more durable style of collar for a larger, stronger pet. With larger dogs the weight of the collar and lead may be less important than the weight of the dog. If your dog tends to pull you can get special leads with padded handles, which are more comfortable for you to hold.

A collar should ride high on your dog's neck, not loose so it slides down to his shoulder blades. For your dog's safety a collar should not be so tight that it will restrict his breathing or cause coughing, or so loose that it will slip over his head. Collar size should be checked frequently on growing puppies. A collar should have a nametag attached to it at all times.

HARNESSES

These are a great alternative to an ordinary collar, and they have many advantages. If you have a smaller dog you can be safe in the knowledge that no pressure is being put on his delicate neck. A harness is also safer for a bigger dog that has a tendency to pull, because it transfers the strain to his shoulders and away from his neck. Some harnesses are designed to prevent your dog from pulling at all.

You can buy matching harness and lead sets in a range of colours and patterns, so your dog's sense of style certainly does not need to be compromised.

SAFETY COLLARS

Unfortunately, the weather is not always fine when you take your dog for a walk, and you may often find yourselves out in foggy or wet conditions. You probably also sometimes walk your dog late in the evening when it's dark. There are many collars and leads available that are fluorescent or that have flashing lights on them to make sure your dog can be seen at all

times, even from long distances (see opposite). This will give you peace of mind when you are walking by the road, and if you let your dog off the lead in poor visibility the collar will allow you to keep your eye on him.

Collars to beware

Among the dazzling array of collars available lurk those that need to be avoided. Prong collars, choke chains, electric shock collars (sometimes called static collars) and slip collars, which tighten around the dog's neck, are all potentially harmful to your dog's health and welfare. While these punitive devices are sold as training aids, they are regarded as forms of abuse by many trainers, and they are never a substitute for kind, consistent and reward-based training.

MAGNETIC COLLARS

These are designed to bring relief from the pain of arthritis and other ailments, without (or together with) the use of drugs. Magnetic fields are said to improve circulation, which enhances the body's ability to heal itself. Increased blood flow to the affected area should promote healing, reduce swelling and give pain relief to arthritic and stiff joints and muscular complaints. The increased blood flow should also help improve the condition of your dog's coat.

PHONE HOME

If you have ever worried about your dog being lonely while you are out of the house, being able to talk to him over the phone will put both your minds at rest. The dog phone (see above), which is attached to his collar, enables constant two-way communication between you and your dog. If your dog ever gets lost, the built-in GPS tracker device will help you to find him again, and if someone else finds him first, they just have to press a single button and the phone will automatically dial home.

Some phones have an in-built temperature gauge, which lets you know when your dog is too hot or too cold. There is also a remote programmable geo-fence capability, which allows you to program certain areas as 'off-limits' and informs you if your dog has gone somewhere he shouldn't have!

THE FUTURE

What will our pampered pooches be wearing in the future? There are designs underway for an electronic 'journal', which can be placed on your dog's collar and which will store information about both you and your dog, including name, address, phone number, vet's visits and medications. A 'fire alert' collar has been proposed that will help firemen to locate a dog in the event of a house fire, and it's even possible to watch your dog via video link when you're not at home!

People and services to pamper your pooch

Some dogs just demand more from life than others. If you are struggling to find enough time and energy to give your pet the very best, why not employ the services of a professional? After all, we think nothing of calling a taxi or making use of the services of a personal trainer, so why shouldn't your dog benefit from such expertise?

DOG WALKERS

When you buy a dog you make a commitment to exercise him yourself, and if you really think that you won't be able to spend at least an hour every day walking your dog you should think twice about getting one. A puppy that is handed over to a dog walker will bond with his walker, not with you.

However, circumstances change, and if you find that work commitments suddenly leave you little spare time or if you become physically unable to take your dog for his regular walks, perhaps it's time to think about getting professional help so that you know that your dog is getting the exercise that he needs.

You may find advertisements for dog-walking services in your local newspaper or directory, on the notice board of your veterinary surgery, or even on the Internet. When choosing a dog walker ask plenty of questions about where they will walk your dog, how long they expect to be out and how many other dogs they walk at the same time. Walking too many dogs at the same time is a form of crowd control rather than the one-on-one attention and training that your dog deserves. A professional dog walker should also be properly insured.

Finally, make sure that the dog walker will stick to your methods of training – it is very frustrating to realize that your dog is being 'detrained' in your absence after all your hard work!

PET TAXIS

Not everyone owns a car, and even if you do it may not always be convenient to drive your dog around. Pet taxis and even limousine services are the answer. While you are at work, your dog can be safely transported from your house, to the groomer, to a dog walker and then to the dog day crèche. Your pooch may end up leading a more active and fulfilling social life than you do!

DAY CRÈCHE

If you are at work all day and are worried about the amount of time your dog is spending on his own, how about putting him into a day crèche? At these centres he will be occupied and entertained all day long and have the chance to spend time with other dogs. You will need to be able to prove that your dog has up-to-date vaccinations before you join.

A word of caution before you decide that this is the best way for your dog to spend the day. If he gets used to spending all day every day playing freely with other dogs, the next time you take him to the park, do not be surprised if he goes charging off to play with the first dog he sees. You may need to step up your training to counteract this.

GROOMERS

Sending your dog to be professionally groomed is a great way to pamper him. A professional groomer will do everything for your dog, from bathing and brushing to nail cutting and ear cleaning. Many groomers now offer a mobile service: they will come to your own home with everything needed for a head-to-tail service. Look at the notice board in your vet's waiting room or check in your local directory for a top-notch groomer. As with all these services, a recommendation from a breeder, close friend, or your veterinary surgeon is the best way to find a reliable service.

just a one-hour walk each day, you might want to consider an au pair. Like the au pairs who are employed to look after children, the canine equivalent will live in your house like another member of the family. Although your arrangement with them may include doing some chores, such as housework and shopping, their primary role is to look after your dog. This would include walking him every day and also grooming and training. Most importantly, they spend time with your dog when you are unable to. Don't forget that a puppy or young dog will tend to bond with the person who spends most time with him, so an au pair is really only suitable for older dogs.

COMPLEMENTARY THERAPISTS

Increasing numbers of vets and dog-lovers are training in the art of complementary therapy, offering a more holistic approach to your dog's health and wellbeing. These services include acupuncture, aromatherapy, chiropractic, herbal and homeopathic remedies and massage, and some of these therapies are described in more detail on pages 74–95. The art of feng shui for dogs, which can be used to enhance their living space, is discussed on pages 22–23. No matter how much faith you have in complementary therapy, nothing should replace a consultation with your vet if you have any doubt at all about your dog's health.

DOG HOTELS

If you are going away on holiday without your dog, you will want to be certain that you have left him in the best possible care. Knowing that your dog is enjoying his own holiday means that you will be able to relax on yours. At a pet hotel your dog will have his own room with all the comforts of the home environment, including such luxuries as his own bed and sofa. Hotels will make sure that your dog enjoys the company of people and other dogs and is well exercised and fed, but some also offer

PET SITTERS

When you go away and are not able to take your dog with you, rather than sending him to a kennel, why not consider hiring a pet sitter? Some sitters will come to your home and stay while you are away, thereby causing as little disruption to your dog as possible. This also gives you the added benefit of knowing your house is being looked after.

Alternatively, some sitters will take your dog into their own home to look after, offering a home-from-home service. Choose your pet-sitter carefully, especially when handing the keys of your house over to someone who is, effectively, a complete stranger.

CANINE AU PAIRS

If you and your family lead busy lives and would like to provide more company for your dog than complementary therapies, such as massage, hydrotherapy and grooming. Some hotels will even try to solve any training issues you may be having while you are away.

PERSONAL TRAINERS

If you are having training problems with your dog – failing to stop him from pulling you like a steam train on the way to the park, for example, or finding that he suffers from a selective hearing problem when he spots another dog – you could consider hiring a dog trainer. A few one-to-one sessions will be much more beneficial than a group session in dealing with any specific problems you are having because the session will be designed specifically to meet the needs of you and your dog. Personal recommendation from a breeder or a friend is the best way to find a good trainer.

SHRINKS

It's not just humans who suffer from stress and depression; your dog can, too. If you are worried about any aspect of his conduct, from his being unable to be left alone at home to his displaying obsessive behaviour such as chasing his tail, consult a qualified pet behaviour counsellor. Some owners put these behaviours down to sheer naughtiness, but it may be that there is another explanation, which a trained counsellor will be able to tease out and remedy.

Buyer beware

When you are choosing any service for your dog, do your research first. Ask for references, speak to other dog owners they work for and, wherever possible, go and watch them at work. Make sure you are completely happy with the service they are offering you and, above all, your dog.

CAPTURING THE MOMENT

It can sometimes be difficult to capture your dog's true personality using a standard camera. This is partly because many dogs find it stressful to have a foreign and unfamiliar object such as a camera held in front of their face. So, for a lasting memento of your dog's unique appearance and character you might want to take him to a photographer who is experienced in animal photography.

A professional photographer will make sure that your dog is given the chance to explore the studio environment before shooting begins so that he is put at ease. He will also consider lighting, background colour and texture and the positioning of your dog to really capture his essence. Whether you want an action shot or a more thoughtful portrait, a professional photographer can really make the difference.

Index

accessories 114–15
acupuncture 91
Afghan Hounds 67, 70, 73
age-related problems 88, 91
agility training 16, 52–3, 56–7, 109
air travel 29
aromatherapy 74, 75–6
arteries 77
arthritis 91, 117, 121

balls 48–9, 86
    activity 105
Basset Hounds 62
bathing 64–5, 87
beaches 27
Beagles 18, 47
Beaucerons 69
beauty therapies 96–101
bed, dog's 13, 22, 23, 24–5
Bergamascos 72
Bichon Frisées 63, 67
bladder weakness 91
bowls 116–17
bows 114
Boxers 19, 21, 47, 66
Briards 70
buster cubes 105

canine au pairs 124
cardiovascular workout 91
celebrations, recipes for 44–5
Chihuahuas 63
children 20
Chinese Crested Dogs 71
chocolates 31
circulation 77, 78, 88, 99, 121
clothes 110–113
Cocker Spaniels 62, 97
collars 118–21
Collies 17
    Bearded 73
    Border 21
complementary therapists 124
crates 25, 26, 28, 29
crossbreeds 19
cruciate ligament rupture 91
Curly Coated Retrievers 72
cycling 47

Dachshunds 18
Dalmations 19, 47
dancing with your dog 54–5
Dandie Dinmonts 70
day crèche 123
days out 26–7, 109
deep breathing 87
dental hygiene 11
dental treatment 100
dew claws 69
diet 58
dog guards 26
dog hotels 124–5
dog phones 121
dog ramps 117
dog walkers 122
doggles 115
dysplasia 91

ear health 62, 123
effleurage 78–9, 83
essential oils 75–6
exercise 10, 11, 12, 46–59
    alternatives to walking 52–5
    enjoying your outings 48–51
    how far and when 47
    on-lead fun 56–7
    the over-pampered pooch 58–9
    relaxation 86
exfoliation 98
eye health 63

family: dog as a family member 8–9
fat camps 59
feng shui 22–3
flyball competitions 53, 109
food 11, 15, 17, 30–45
    active dog/couch potato 31
    allergies/intolerances 32, 36
    complementary 31
    complete 31, 92
    cooked bones 32
    eating in peace 20, 21
    feeding frequency 31
    food circuits 50–51
    food problems 32–3
    healthy snacks for training 34–5
    human food 31

recipes for celebrations 44–5
recipes for meals 36–9
recipes for treats 40–43
scattering 105
supersized dogs 33
when travelling 26, 27
see also nutrients
fracture repair 91

games 13, 16, 17, 48–51, 86, 108, 109
    brain games to play indoors 102–3
    keeping your dog alert 104–5
German Shepherd Dogs 19, 67
Golden Retrievers 47, 67
Greyhounds 18, 86
Griffons Bruxellois 73
groomers 123
grooming 66–7
gundogs 17

hair clips 114
hair-dyes 67
hairstyles 70–73
happy dogs
    breeds 16–19
    canine smiles 14
    ears 14, 15
    lust for life 14–15
    play bow 14
    tail wagging 14, 15
    telltale signs 15
harnesses 26, 120
health spas 59
herding breeds 17, 51
holidays 28–9
holistic therapy 90–93
    acupuncture 91
    hydrotherapy 91
    nutrition 92–3
home environment 12, 20–21
hounds 18, 47
hydrotherapy 91

immune system 78
injuries 88, 91
Irish Setters 73
Irish Terriers 73
Irish Wolfhounds 73

Italian Greyhounds 18

Jack Russells 16, 47
jacuzzi 87–8
jewellery 114
joint problems 87, 91

King Charles Spaniels 18
King Kong 104
Komondors 72
Kong dispensers 117

Labradoodles 70, 71
Labradors 21, 47, 86
lactic acid 83
leads
    and cycling 47
    etiquette 57
    on-lead fun 56–7
    and walking 47
lymphatic system 78, 83

massage 68, 74, 75
    for the active dog 77–9
    post-walk 83–5
    pre-walk 80–82
    scalp 99
meals, recipes for 36–9
mental activity 13
mobility problems 87
mongrels 19
music 68, 89

nail trimming and polishing 68–9,
    123
new babies 108
new puppies 21, 109
new routine 109
noise 20, 21
nutrition 92–3

obesity 33, 58–9, 91
Old English Sheepdogs 70, 73
orthopaedic conditions 91
osteochondrosis 91
owners
    body language 7
    what your dog does for you 8

pain management 91
paws: health 63
Pekingeses 71
personal trainers 125
pet behaviour counsellors 125
pet carriers 27, 28, 116
pet passports 29
pet sitters 124
pet taxis 123
Petometer 47
photographer 125
plastic surgery 59
Pomeranians 67, 97
Poodles 63, 67, 70, 71, 72
Portuguese Water Dogs 67, 70, 71,
    72
Pugs 66
Pyrenean Mountain Dogs 69, 86

qi 91

recipes see food
reflexology 89
reiki 94
relaxation 74, 83, 99
    deep breathing 87
    deep relaxation 89
    exercise 86
    jacuzzi 87–8
    reflexology 89
    yoga 88
rheumatism 91
running 47
Russian Black Terriers 73

St Bernards 86
scent hounds 18
scent trail 57
Schnauzers 67, 71, 73
    Miniature 47
Schnoodles 70, 71
Siberian Husky, needs of 19
sight hounds 18, 86
skin conditions 91
sleep 13, 20, 21, 22, 23
slimming clubs 58
snacks see food
social skills 13, 51

special occasions 67, 68
spray conditioners 67
stiffness 78, 83, 121
stroke sufferers 91
sun cream 111
surgery 91, 111
swimming 54, 87, 91

tags 115
teeth 61, 100
Tellington Touch 94, 95
Tellington-Jones, Linda 95
tents, pop-up 26
terrier types 16
total hip replacement 91
toy dogs 18
toys 11, 16, 17, 21, 25, 47, 49, 50,
    103, 104, 105
training 11, 17, 122
    agility 16, 52–3, 56–7, 109
    groundwork for fun 51
    healthy snacks for 34–5, 51
    personal trainers 125
travel bags 116
travel sickness 26
travelling 26–9, 116
treats 11, 25, 26, 30, 49, 50, 62, 66,
    68, 86
    chase the treat 105
    recipes for 40–43
tricks 11, 13, 16, 106–7, 108

vaccinations 29, 123
veins 78, 83
veterinary check-ups 11

walking 11, 12, 15, 17, 21, 27, 47,
    48, 108, 109, 122
water, drinking 32, 117
water therapy 87–8
West Highland Terriers 16, 47
Whippets 18
working trials 53, 109

yoga 88
Yorkshire Terriers 18, 67, 70, 73, 97

Acknowledgements

The publisher would like to thank the following people for their contributions to this book:

Sarah Whitehead of **Alpha Pet Behaviour**
www.dogtrain.co.uk

Ann Lees, consultant of the **Feng Shui Society**
www.fengshuisociety.org.uk

Ryan O'Meara of **K9 Magazine**
www.k9magazine.com

Jill Blair of **Jilly B's**
www.jillybs.org.uk

Julia Robertson of **Galen Therapy Centre**
www.caninetherapy.co.uk

Executive Editor Trevor Davies
Editor Leanne Bryan
Executive Art Editor Darren Southern
Designer Maggie Town, One2Six Creative
Illustrations Sudden Impact Media
Production Controller Nigel Reed
Picture Library Manager Sophie Delpech

The publisher would like to thank the following for the loan of props for photography:

The Company of Animals
(see pages 56 and 117 bottom)
www.companyofanimals.co.uk
+44 (0) 1932 566 696

Pet Company
(see page 5 bottom)
www.petcompany.co.uk
+44 (0) 1142 620 370

Pet London
(see pages 110 and 115 bottom)
www.petlondon.net
+44 (0) 20 7580 7580

Pets and the City
(see pages 12, 28, 29, 33, 111, 113 top right, 114, 115 top, 119 top and bottom, 120)
www.petsandthecityuk.com
+44 (0) 20 8858 3527

PetsMobility
(see page 121)
www.petsmobility.com
+1 (480) 344 7724

Pucci Petwear
(see page 115)
www.puccipetwear.com
+44 (0) 1825 760 200

Seapets
(see page 116)
www.seapets.co.uk
+44 (0) 845 230 4777

The Dog Boutique
(see pages 25, 31, 32, 112, 113 bottom left, 117 top, 125)
www.thedogboutique.co.uk
+44 (0) 870 803 4806